Redemption

Redemption

◆

a tale of two worlds

KARIN JOHANNE BOER

iUniverse, Inc.
New York Lincoln Shanghai

Redemption
a tale of two worlds

iUniverse books may be ordered through booksellers or by contacting:

iUniverse
2021 Pine Lake Road, Suite 100
Lincoln, NE 68512
www.iuniverse.com
1-800-Authors (1-800-288-4677)

ISBN-13: 978-0-595-38894-3 (pbk)
ISBN-13: 978-0-595-83272-9 (ebk)
ISBN-10: 0-595-38894-9 (pbk)
ISBN-10: 0-595-83272-5 (ebk)

Printed in the United States of America

Dedicated
To My Children
and
Grandchildren

In Honor
of
My Father

Contents

Acknowledgements

It is said that no book is produced by a lone effort. Mine has been accompanied by both professional and non-professional encouragers. I extend thanks deeper than words to my husband, Wally, whose faith in this project never flagged, no matter how many trees worth of paper went into the wastebasket. My editors, Kathy Ide and Tricia Mathys, gave me invaluable professional help. My dear friend and published author, Barbra Minar, gave persistent affirmation from beginning to end, without which I couldn't have proceeded.

Special thanks to my brother, Erling, who without even knowing of my project sent the gift of a painstakingly translated letter written by my sister to Norwegian relatives in 1945, celebrating the end of the war in Europe. He had no idea how valuable this letter would be to this work. Thank you, my brother.

Digging deeply into stored memories, especially those from early childhood, presents some hazards: what is remembered by me may not line up with what is remembered by others who were there and know better. I offer this acknowledgement especially to Erling, and my cousin, Bjørn, whose recollections are different and sharper, stored in memories at least nine years older than mine. For whatever fictionalization appears in the recounting of the war years and of later family relationships, I apologize. I can tell only my own story.

Some names have been changed. Otherwise, the story is true, as are the characters portrayed. The beauty and power of their lives helped to form and change mine forever.

PART I

The Setup

1

Ghosts Revisited

My father used to say you can never go back. By that I assumed he meant you can't go back to the home you were turned out of or the town you fled, and no other meaning ever occurred to me until I began to write this sentence. Did he really mean something merely philosophical, like never being able to go back to live your life differently or going back to try to make things right that were done wrong? In any case, the only meaning I ever attributed to his stark announcement was that he—not me or some generalized somebody—could never go back to where he came from, which was not just a home he was thrown out of but an entire country. When he stated emphatically that he would never go back to Norway I believed him, for he said it as one who wouldn't willingly return to hell fire.

Nevertheless, I had to try this "going back" myself once or twice before realizing that he was right. Nothing was the same, of course, not even the feelings I expected to re-enact like an encore. And when the place, or place in time, had been marked by as much pain as pleasure, the visitation was attended by a certain sensation of masochism, along with the childishly simple question: why am I doing this?

The last time I tried to prove his hypothesis wrong, I attempted to go back in time about twenty years to a place that had once brought enchantment, love, then betrayal and a kind of terror.

It is a Saturday, and I am on my way to the beach. When I impulsively turn right off of Sunset Boulevard and head up toward Angelo Drive, high above the Beverly Hills homes where I spent much of my later childhood, I couldn't have told you what I thought I would accomplish. Of course it was partly in search of remembered beauty: the road wound up through the wealthiest, most extravagantly landscaped mansions in Southern California, and I always loved the drive itself.

But this day I feel like I am winding through more than the predictable 'June gloom' that creeps ashore from the Pacific each year; there is, progressively, a sad

3

heaviness in the air. Smog, too, of course, all eerily blended with imaginary ghosts from the big house on the hill. Cypress and ornamental pines recede into the background along the road like a faded movie set. I find myself driving more cautiously than necessary along the stately, curving street and I wonder: if I could focus my eyes just right, would I be able to see the unsubstantial figures of Gisela and Karl, Meredeth and Penn, standing like wraithlike sentinels at the bottom of the long driveway leading to the Von Breuner mansion? They would probably mutter irritably, *"Go home. You don't belong here anymore."*

Even as I proceed, I know that is true. But I also know that turning around is out of the question.

I do have the sense to know I dare not inch the car to the top. That would be plain trespassing now, and I am saddened by the thought. So I park near the bottom of the driveway and let the car idle as I strain to envision the wide, graveled parking lot above.

Once, the mansion beyond had been the weekly party place for students from U.C.L.A., and flashy, chromed autos of the mid '40's filled every available inch of parking space. Tuxedoed young men politely disembarked their fur-wrapped girlfriends, one shiny black shoe on the running board, manicured feminine hands extended, waiting.

A wave of nostalgia engulfs me as I consider that now that same sweep of gravel might now be bastioned with the cars of strangers who would call the police if I went much farther. So I settle at the base of the driveway in my white 1975 Mustang coupe, motor running, remembering.

Gisela, the matriarch of the Von Bruener family stands regally by the massive front door dispensing gardenias to each of the perfectly coifed young collegiates as they file through the foyer to the ball. Gardenias by the hundreds border the entire frontage of the house. On either side of the door sultry white blossoms are massed in profusion in a wicker basket and fill the air with exotic perfume. She smiles. Her dark eyes glitter.

I sigh to think of it. Gardenias and a Von Breuner ball will be forever linked with that torridly romantic time period. I wonder if the gardenias are still there. Gisela is gone. Most likely the rest of the Von Breuner ghosts have abandoned their posts at windows and doors. What I should really worry about is the new, very alive owner.

As I sit alert and upright in the car I wonder what it would be like to be caught as a trespasser on property that now belongs to a famous movie star. The house, a grand duplicate of the Von Breuner's summerhouse in Bremen, remained on the market for years after Gisela's and Karl's deaths. When the young celebrity bought it I was shocked. I could have accepted an old European couple quietly carrying on the aristocratic tradition of the house. But a sophisticated Hollywood actress? What would she do with the twenty-some rooms, not including the attic and dungeon? What will she do when chill winds begin snaking from room to room, leftover spirits searching for a séance to attend? I am worried about her.

I move the car forward a little and squint up at the house. It is so overgrown with ivy the second-story windows are hidden. Oh, how I want to drive up there, walk in the front door as I used to almost every weekend during the school year and for weeks at a time during the summer. I would slip into the cool, polished-wood foyer with the massive oak spiral staircase off to the right and sneak quietly up the stairs. I would plant my feet right on that Persian rug that ran the length of the long hallway, the one I'd always been warned to keep my shoes off of. I'd peek into every one of the five bedroom suites, each with their own library, fire-place, dressing room and bath. Then I'd walk straight into Meredeth's room, across the marbled hearth to the casement windows. I would stand there and greedily take in the view that had never ceased to fill me with wonder: the sweep of the Los Angeles coastline to the south, its curve northward to Malibu. If it was a clear day I would see San Pedro, the top of UCLA's Royce Hall through the trees, and boats like toys sitting in the endless blue of Santa Monica's sea.

From Meredeth's room, where I spent so much time in intense conversation with her in front of the fireplace or reading in solitude from her expansive library curled up on the cushioned window seat, it is a short walk down the hall to the narrow stairs that curve down to the kitchen. That kitchen was like none I had seen before or since. Several chefs could cook there at once, utilizing the two stoves, two refrigerators, two sinks, and miles of countertops. It wore me out just walking the distance to make a sandwich. But oh, the joy of it. I can almost hear Meredeth's lilting voice issuing instructions as I made my first attempt at a German *linzertorte*. But it was the magic in her California salads that eluded me. I never could get the proportions right between the dribble of olive oil, the dash of wine vinegar, the sprinkling of garlic salt, and ground black pepper. She *must* have wickedly thrown in something else when I wasn't looking. Things were not always as they appeared with Meredeth; being mysterious about everything she did was her personal code.

Trees rustle behind the car. I jump, but there is no one. My eyes search out the row of lower story windows that open to the servants' quarters. In my mind I stroll down the hallway past them to the sunlit laundry and sewing room—even on gloomy days the windows on all three sides made it ablaze with light. I had always wanted time to stop there, pick up one of the bolts of fabric in the wicker basket, spread a pattern onto the long cutting table under the window overlooking the herb garden, and settle down to make a dress, or at least a skirt. If Meredeth hadn't kept me so busy reading theosophy and occult mysticism in her bedroom, I would gladly have spent my days in the sewing room. I could see the untouched baskets of brightly colored yarns and the unused spinning wheel standing in the corner under a window to the west. Before Gisella had become a rather alarming person I would have loved to ask her to teach me the art of weaving. Table runners maybe, ones like my mother had crafted and sent to us wrapped in tissue paper from her home in a Norwegian hospital.

Why, I wonder, had that wonderfully equipped room been so little used? I had met the Von Brueners only a year after the war was over, mid-summer of '46. They had to have been at one time very wealthy. Had the war with Germany changed everything? Maybe the maids' rooms had been occupied and the sewing room a bustle of activity before then. Had they, as Germans—titled, at that, for they were *baron* and *baroness* (something that made me feel, by association, insufferably proud)—experienced post-war humiliations in their Beverly Hills villa?

A black car crawls up the road toward me and I hold my breath. What if it is *her*? I am practically blocking the driveway and my heart pounds. But I manage to casually ease the car around to roll on down the street, ready to explain I have simply been lost. The black car passes, turns a corner, and disappears. I can still see the house from my vantage point, but I dare not mentally roam any more of its rooms. It really is time to get myself out of here…

And yet a memory of eating at their twelve-foot dining table with a large party of jovial guests makes me hesitate. It was one of the Sundays when the Von Brueners threw a brunch, easily seating twenty people or more around the massive oak table. Candlesticks the size of Corinthian columns stood atop it on a long, hand-woven runner. The imperious Gisela always sat at the end near the fireplace, rosy and sharp eyed with steel-gray hair escaping as if electrically charged from a tightly wound bun on top of her head. A great ceramic bowl was filled to the top with homemade waffle batter. She poured, baked, served, and poured again until the guests groaned in satisfaction. Without embarrassment I always ate more than everyone else so was always last to finish—but this time I looked up to see everyone staring at me with amusement. "That girl has no bottom," someone said, and everyone laughed. One at a time they pushed their plates full of scraps of bacon, German sausages, and uneaten scrambled eggs toward me. I sat, mouth full and face hot, surrounded by a semicircle of other people's leftovers. "This little Norwegian girl is a glutton, it seems," a deep male voice commented slyly. Again came laughter…

The sun is burning through the gloom and the steering wheel is hot to the touch. My hands feel clammy. How long have I been sitting here? It really *is* time to go. I release the parking break and ask myself how in the world had it happened that I had been ushered, a mere ten-year old child, into the unconventional world inside this mansion in the first place? The complexity of conflicting recollections—happiness and revulsion—shadow my recall, as always. Memories sparkling with promise plunge beneath a black pool of disillusionment.

It is just a house now, I think. Its story is probably forgotten to everyone but me (I can't help but believe I am the only one left alive of that generation; but, of course, that is pure conjecture, with maybe some wishful thinking thrown in). I wouldn't want to meet any Von Bruener who has outlived this place. Who of them would believe what a pivotal influence their house had once been in my life, requiring what heroic rescue? That it was haunted I had no doubt—not haunted as others are alleged to be, due to accident or murder, but a deliberate, invited haunting to present a show of spiritual power because earthly power had been lost.

One thing I know: no matter what those losses had been, the Von Breuners and their daughter, Meredeth, had remained proud, gregarious, seductively overbearing in their generosity and warmth to the end of my relationship with them. While they lived and gave, mesmerized and manipulated, romanced and seduced, nothing and no one could quite resist them.

I turn the key in the ignition and slowly begin the winding descent down Angelo Road. The big house shrinks behind the massive trees atop the drive and appears as a mere rooftop. I know, as I stop to turn west on Sunset Boulevard, that I will never drive up Angelo Drive again. That part of my 'going back' is over.

2

To Set the Stage

If my sister, Kirsten, had met Meredeth when they were both thirteen, they would have had nothing at all in common besides their age.

In 1937, Meredeth is having her first flirtatious encounters with men while on a family cruise on the Mediterranean and loses her girlhood (or gives it away, which is more likely) somewhere between New York and Crete. Kirsten, meanwhile, is in Norway receiving the announcement that she has a new baby sister, and that neither mother nor baby will be coming home from the hospital anytime soon. While Meredeth's horizons are expanding beyond her southern California mansion with adventures beyond her age, Kirsten's are closing in on her within the walls of a house overlooking the *Oslofjord*, squeezing her young life dry with fear and grief.

Meredeth and Kirsten won't be sharing their childhood stories until their paths cross in Los Angeles seven years later. Then, as they compare travel experiences, their very incompatibility draws them together and they become best friends, to everyone's surprise and not a little suspicion. The contrast in their appearance makes every head turn: Kirsten, pale blonde with soft blue eyes and shy smile; Meredeth, regal with thick black hair and fiery dark eyes that hold others almost against their will. (How well I remember that hold.) Kirsten, reserved and cautious with words, seems content to let Meredeth speak for her. When strategic social occasions arise Meredeth is vocal enough for them both.

A long seven years will go by before Meredeth makes her flamboyant entrance into our little home and more or less takes over our lives. In the meantime, there is some history I need to ferret out, and the only one I can I direct my unsettling questions to is my sister. I learn the vagaries of our peculiar family in a series of 'bathroom vignettes'. When getting out of the tub, shivering in front of the glowing electric heater on the wall, brushing my teeth, watching her brush her hair, I ask impudent questions Kirsten is forced to answer before she has a convenient escape.

She puts her comb down and frowns, leans against the wall with arms crossed in front. She is becoming adept at putting a good face on things.

"Why don't we have a mother?" I ask.

"We do have one. She's just not with us."

"Where is she?"

"She's still in Norway, where you were born. In a hospital."

"What's wrong with her?"

"She's…got a mental illness. She's in a world of her own." It takes some doing to explain this phenomenon to me, but she never gets far beyond that simple equation.

Kirsten grabs a towel and rubs me down hard. I look at my feet, red toes curled around the loose bath mat. I can't see her face, but I know she is frowning. I can feel it in the way she pushes the towel around quickly over my shoulders, down my legs, as if to get the job over with and away from this hopeless talk.

"I don't remember her," I persist. I feel my heart thudding against my ribs as I twist around to shed the towel.

"Well, you never knew her." She hands me my pajamas.

"Is she very sick?"

"She was sick before you were born."

"Will she get better?"

She takes a deep breath. "No. Here's your brush." She then kneels by the tub and begins mopping it down with rapid swipes of the towel. "She's not unhappy, Karin. She's really very well taken care of." I try to imagine this. With those words her condition sounds pleasant enough. At about this point I gaze at myself in the mirror and wonder what my mother looks like.

"What was she like before she got sick?" I wonder aloud. I feel confused. Had the sickness made her happier? That's how Kirsten makes it sound.

"She was beautiful," she says. "Lighthearted and lovely. She loved to sing, just like you. She was kind and cheerful." She watches me as I brush my wet hair and studies me in the mirror. "You and she are very much alike," she remarks.

This statement, made frequently, always makes her voice seem kind of strained, and I am strangely afraid to ask her what she means.

You have probably experienced yourself what I felt then and later as it was repeated during the course of my childhood. A statement meant to assure rings in your head with an attached foreboding that was never intended. But it resounds very much like the dreaded "You'll never amount to anything," or "You are just like your father," who happens to be a bum or an alcoholic. At those words, *You and she are very much alike,* the dreamy state in which I fantasize my mother as being nearly angelic is rudely awakened. I drop the brush and we bump heads as we both stoop to pick it up. What does it *mean* that I am like my mother? Lovely—sick—mentally off—cheerfully singing—hospitalized a continent away and *happy* in a world of her own?

"She's one of the hardest cases in the hospital there," Kirsten says, "and so far there's no cure for it." Far from softening my misgivings, this lends the whole story a romance that no such story should have. A tragic heroine. However, it is far more preferable to envision my phantom mother being beautiful and singing cheerfully in some far off land, and with that I get on with brushing my teeth.

It is understood that these little conversations with Kirsten are only to be between us. My father never speaks of Mother. Neither does our brother, Erling, at least not in my presence. At times I feel sulkily as though all the history of my family is locked away in another world and I would be the worst, most insolent of intruders to try to go there.

◆   ◆   ◆

It is my father's secret past I am most determined to unearth. Quietly, with an intensity that spans all the years that follow, I carefully arrange the puzzle pieces I am given. They are dropped haphazardly, as if no one knows I'm watching or listening, so I assemble them with stealth.

It is romantic to learn that Father and Mother had met in Norway in 1918 while singing in a choir concert tour. It is exciting to think this remote and depressed middle-aged man had won his architectural degree in Norway and that his sculptures and paintings are still hanging in the university there. I am enthralled to think that he was an adventurous youth and that when he wanted to travel he became a steward on a ship bound for Greece from the North Atlantic where storms raged and everybody was sick and some fell overboard. I admire the courage that drove him to take photos showing the deck of the ship deeply angled against the waves, passengers gray of face and hanging on to the side, sprayed with angry foam while he kept his sea-legs and earned his way to America. How amazing that this faded figure of a man had once traveled all over the country, working odd jobs from east to west, in watermelon fields in the South (where he discovered he was violently allergic to watermelons), then as a prune picker on an orchard in Oregon. Then, in 1920 he discovered the beauty of southern California. "Orange groves," he once reminisced to no one in particular after a couple of martinis. "Nothing but orange groves. God's country then." He didn't embellish the remark, but returned to his drink in a silent, disillusioned reverie.

Have you ever waited long enough to hear an old man, known for being one of few words, finally honor you with just a few treasured reminiscences? You hang onto every word and pray no one in the room will interrupt with something silly like "Oh, how very interesting," or "My goodness, what happened then?" For you know that would dam up the flow of riches right now and there won't be another trickle for months.

How I loved these brief, infrequent glimpses into my father's shrouded past! I felt it would be impudent to ask anything outright, so I stayed quietly alert for those moments when someone outside the family incautiously prodded on past his reserve. It was always after dinner, following his quiet, elaborate ritual of tamping, filling, and lighting his pipe. Sometimes the only reward for those guests was a clamped-down silence. It all depended on who *they* were. I sometimes caught him give a triumphant half-smile behind their backs as they simply got up, said good-night, and left.

At some point my mother displayed her 1920's woman's audacity and followed him to the United States, determining to make the roving, artistic bachelor her own. They got married in Beverly Hills. But I am appalled to think how this happened. How could any man so rooted and grounded in disdain for females possibly ever have been glad to have been aggressively pursued and caught by a woman? By Kirsten's account they had been deeply in love, but it doesn't square with me that he could have loved her all that much and act the way he does toward women (namely my sister and me) now! He is a closed gate to us, his daughters, and a tower of disapproval to his son.

From that sad observation I develop a secret internal doctrinal statement: *Men are women haters at heart.*

My parents traveled back and forth during the twenties, living in Norway for a time, then returning to live in various towns near Los Angeles. I heard this much from Kirsten herself: she was born in Beverly Hills during one stay; Erling was born in Glendora during another, escorted by fire engines through a downtown firestorm on his way to the hospital. (Somehow, as I got to know my brother, that seemed fitting.) It was to be providential to a high degree that this made my brother and sister American rather than Norwegian citizens.

What my father was doing for a living during this period no one ever said. But I could tell from the photos found in dark, dusty little albums that they lived well, played hard, and went on weekend camping trips. Once, while sitting on the floor paging through the pictures, Kirsten appears over my shoulder and tells me they had owned a cabin in the Tehachapi mountains with another couple, spending nights playing cards and drinking home-brewed liquor. Dad made a lot of beer during prohibition.

"Oh, come on, Dad. Tell Karin the snake story," Kirsten says that evening over the clacking of her knitting needles. At twenty-one she is knitting like her life depends on it and makes huge, elaborately designed ski sweaters for boys she is interested in impressing. She seems to be in a careless mood, her plain brown cotton skirt scrunched up around her knees, her sandaled feet crossed over each other, her hands flying, needles flashing above the bulk of dark blue knit mashed down in her lap. She wears an impatient frown as if fed up with all the secrecy in our lives. I seize the moment and settle in to stare him down until he decides to come forth. He eyes me as if assessing how long I will hold out. I refuse to move. He slowly empties and fills his pipe, and I hold my breath as the match flame licks his thumb before he flings it in the ashtray.

He sags a bit in the chair, defeated by our determination, and commences the storytelling. Soon it is as if he is reliving and relishing every detail. My surprise at this borders on alarm. Will he really continue? I freeze in position.

And so he begins: One morning after a long, hard night of partying he had ventured out of the cabin at dawn and bolted in terror at what he saw. Hundreds of snakes were draped all over the surrounding trees and fences. He edged back into the cabin, screaming in terror to his hung-over companions that he had poisoned himself on liquor and had the DTs. The only sober man of the bunch got out of bed, surveyed the scene from behind bloodshot eyes, turned around and went back to bed. On his way he assured Dad the snakes were real. This was their yearly place to shed their skins. Dad vowed he'd never take another drink, but he lied.

He takes a sip of his whiskey and soda, warmed to his subject and our attentiveness. "So," he continues, "I kept on brewing my own beer, which I stashed in a closet. My friends and I were playing poker one hot summer night when every last bottle blew its cork and sent rivers of beer flowing out under the door." He looks at me with a wry smile and adds, "*That* was what was called 'prohibition' in this country."

My father took his family back to Norway when the depression hit, then went to England in search of work. There was no construction going on in northern Europe, nothing to be done architecturally. Just as he was about broke, he was approached by Vincent and Alexander Korda, film-makers from

Hungary, to design sets and be assistant art director for their burgeoning movie business. He accepted, but grudgingly. He wanted to design fine houses, not film sets. However, once in England he began what became a kind of double life, full of fine hotels, stylish suits, and Havana cigars. "Now *that* was the good life," he says with conviction. But I know it is hot the day of this saying; he has just mowed the lawn and weeded the garden, and is probably tired of his residential chores.

"While he was in England, did he ever visit you and Mother in Norway before the war?" I ask Kirsten privately. We're in the bathroom, getting ready for bed.

"Sometimes," she replies. A bit guardedly, I think.

He must have, I'm thinking, because I was born in the Norwegian hospital in which Mother was to stay, maybe forever. Then he must have returned to his favorite London hotel, designed and painted film sets for movies featuring the greats like Vivian Leigh and Clark Gable until the war broke out.

◆   ◆   ◆

As a child I fantasized about the details of my birthday in the Norwegian spring of 1937—there was no one to describe it to me outside of my own imagination. But perhaps that is what motherless daughters and orphans do—invent origins and design sets for them. It might have been snowy and cold, the first velvety buds of pussy willow (I *do* remember the heartbreaking sweetness of pussy willows) breaking forth, touching frozen white with soft points of downy brown. But more likely it rained continually during the first weeks of April, melting the forbidding landscape into misty grays. In the stubborn fictions of childhood, my birthday was brilliant with spring's first real sunshine, all clear blue and pink and golden, like Easter.

All of Europe was a perilous place those last years of the '30's. As the Nazi invasion swept from Poland into northern Europe, many of my relatives remained near the eye of the storm and were part of the clandestine workings of the Norwegian underground. My father and most family members were strangers to me, for I was placed in a children's home for my first three years, and there my first relationships were with state-appointed nurses. I've since realized that it isn't surroundings but people that build the perceptions of early life. To be torn from the surrogate family ties of infancy means to suffer an intrinsic loss and to experience a stubborn underground grief.

I did not perceive the absence of my father in my life, for he was rarely referred to by anyone. I accepted this mystery as children accept all obscure realities.

There must have been much Kirsten never divulged—or was too emotionally ravaged to even have made note of for anyone else's sake, although I'm aware of a detailed letter she wrote to the family in Norway after we left. Though my curiosity was fervent, how could I have asked her to explain more than she had already offered about my mother's state of mind at the time of my birth? Did she ever hold me? When did they take me away?

Left to my own devices, I wove a ragged and distorted tapestry of our family history. Over dinner or drinks, drawn out of reticent mouths by neighbors or friends too persistent to resist, bits and pieces of what happened to the family were dropped like nuggets. Rarely are these scenarios painted for *me*; I mostly came by them while eavesdropping. But some were visualized with the help of those old, dog-eared photos—dream-like still shots of people, frozen in time, seen in a blur through the thin light of Norwegian winters and the long, low light of Norway at midsummer. They are important to this telling simply because, like my father's film sets, these scenes set the stage for all that would come later.

At an impossibly early moment of my life a numinous memory is etched in my mind—I can still imagine it in all its sweet light; it is no fantasy. From my crib I see the face of a dark-haired woman hovering over me. She is crisply uniformed in white with a dark blue bib and headdress, touched with an embroidered red form of a cross above her forehead. Beyond her are high, wide walls in that particular yellow which will forever characterize Norwegian yellow to me, a real *ochre*, flooded with the long rays of the midsummer sun. The tall windows reach nearly to the high, sloped ceiling. Beneath them, rows of cribs line the walls as far as my eye can see. I look up into her tranquil face and feel her touch my cheek. She closes her eyes and murmurs softly over me: "Our Father, which art in heaven…" I hear it, in that tiny, focused memory, *in English*. But of course, it has to have been spoken in Norwegian.

My nurse's name was Ellen, always referred to respectfully by Kirsten as *Tante* Ellen.

"She loved you as her own child," Kirsten tells me, "Though she broke all the rules to do so. She got into a lot of trouble over you. Favoritism over the babies in the home was not allowed in those days." I could imagine some harassed head nurse saying, "Put that child down, Ellen, she's been fed and changed. Don't forget you are responsible for all the other children." By the time I was three, there must have been many uniformed arms that held and propped, patted and plumped up us orphans with those layers of wool needed during the long winter days and nights.

But Tante Ellen's arms belonged to me.

On a cold spring day in 1940 I am sent to live in Oslo with Onkel Anders, Tante Dagny, and their two children, Bjørn and Kari. My sister's young arms take over where Tante Ellen's leave off. Kirsten looks like a grown-up lady to me, gentle and quiet behind the boisterous noise of the other three children. But at sixteen she is a kind of orphan herself, thrust into a mother role that will last her short lifetime. She is a very serious looking girl.

In some shadowy background, watching and darting, ominously appearing and reappearing like a sly, menacing threat to whatever established peace there could be, is Erling. At twelve he is a restless waif in competition with a sister, two cousins, an unexpected toddler, and an oncoming war. My sister's face is continually frowning, voices around us are sharp and somber, space is cramped and crowded and cold. April is still freezing; spring won't come until June. It is a long winter and everyone is irritable.

But on one unusual morning there is a cheerful bustle in the kitchen. I am watching eagerly over the edge of the kitchen table as Tante Dagny and Kirsten are making a cake. Kari gathers jams and jellies and I watch her trudge up from the basement carrying jars of lingonberries and raspberries. "Don't forget to bring the cream too," Tante Dagny calls. Kari puts the jars on the table and returns to the basement. She wears thick glasses over eyes that are crossed, but smiles and laughs even when everyone else is sullen.

Everything is interrupted by a loud banging on the front door. Tante Dagny wipes her hands on her apron and opens it cautiously, telling all of us to shush. I hide behind Kirsten.

An old man at the door makes an announcement. He is out of breath. "The Nazis have come. The invasion of Norway is upon us. Soldiers will be at our doors any moment. Prepare!" As quickly as he came, he is gone. It is April 9, one day before my third birthday.

"Kari," Tante Dagny whispers shakily. "Take everything back down to the basement!"

From then on there isn't much food at all, only detestable brown fish, herring oil on bread, and cod-liver oil by tablespoons forced into my mouth as many times as it takes before I stop spitting it out and swallow it. We spend our days behind blackout curtains, nights under the siren sounds in the basement; my aunt and uncle showing alert fear in their eyes with every sound. They seem to whisper endlessly.

I know it is a basement, but the word *dungeon* seems more accurate. The cold. The smell. The dark. For two years following the invasion we spend night after night down there, huddled together within its cold, gray stone walls, sleeping on hard benches, bundled in wool blankets but still shivering until our teeth clatter. When the long nights are over, we troop stealthily up the narrow cellar stairs to sit at the big dining table in near darkness to eat a spare breakfast of bread and *gjetøst*, a sweet brown cheese made from goat's milk. The rare mornings when butter accompanies the bread are like dark little parties and the whispering is broken by soft words and quiet laughter.

It is before dawn when the tumult in the streets between Nazi soldiers and outraged Norwegians explodes: the sound of shouts, curses and now a volley of gunshots. Ashen, with beads of sweat standing on their faces, Tante Dagny and Onkel Anders lean around the radio, and soon a voice over the crackling airways announces the dreaded order: *Evacuate the children.* Phones ring, horns blare, air raid sirens scream. Fathers, uncles, and grandfathers swarm the neighborhood, calling for the children to get out of bed and get dressed for travel. With tears coursing down her cheeks, Tante Dagny hastily shoves arms and legs into warm clothing and pushes us out the door with Onkel Anders. He piles us into waiting vehicles—horse carts, trucks, hay wagons, donkeys, and what few cars are available.

Roads narrow into mountain paths. Drivers ditch the stalled cars and trucks and we tumble out to stagger ahead by foot. The ragged band lumbers over rocky heights, trudges through jagged valleys. Men, horses, and mules carry the little ones; the older children herd younger ones like sheep as they stumble along.

By nightfall we come upon a wide, secluded glen. In the midst of a grove of birch there stands an old schoolhouse, a welcome refuge for the exhausted troupe. Several men immediately hike out to scour the region for any source of food. One of them finds a small abandoned mountain store. Another helps break in and loot it, then loads down a mule with all they can carry. Before leaving, he scrawls a note promising to pay for what had been lifted when the war is over, and sticks it in the doorjamb as he pushes the door shut. That man is my father. He has been summoned from somewhere, and he has appeared. But I don't know him.

A farmhouse some ten miles away is the only source of milk. Once the small plunder of stolen rations has been exhausted, milk becomes the sole provision for the next two weeks. Each day before dawn my father and two other men set out by foot for the farm, returning at night with vats of milk suspended on poles slung across their shoulders.

Finally the all-clear signal comes and we begin the long trek home.

But something goes awry after the herds of children are shepherded back into Oslo. "You gave us a lot of trouble," Onkel Anders tells me later with a twinkle in his eye. "All the other children got home safely enough, but you and that donkey of yours disappeared!" A frantic search through streets, woods, and mountain paths...all afternoon weary men hunt for me, fearing the worst. I sit crying, too afraid to move, watching the sun go down behind the trees surrounding me. At last the man I love most (I never loved a man more) appears from behind some brambles. Onkel Anders has spotted the donkey first, placidly eating grass in a small clearing surrounded by firs. He finds me sleeping in the cart, my face tear-streaked and dirty.

"Karin!" he shouts. Relief splits his monkey-like face into crags of laughter. He swoops me up in his thin, strong arms as if never to let me go. He tousles my hair and embraces me so hard I can't breathe. Then, in mock anger he accuses me of playing hide-and-seek with all the elders of Oslo.

The two-story gray house on the wooded hill overlooking Oslofjørd is our home—and prison—for over two years. Early each morning Onkel Anders walks down the long hill to his job at an import-export company near the Oslofjørd while Tante Dagny manages the restless household. We are on constant alert for surprise visits from the *S.S.* They march with their tall leather boots into the kitchen, confiscate food, rudely rifle through desks and drawers and cupboards. They shoot harsh questions at Tante Dagny in German while we stand like statues behind her. She responds with "*Ja*," or "*Nay*," in her low, controlled voice, then stands stiffly aside when they leave, their arms loaded with goods from our household.

The leaden atmosphere of their sudden comings and goings drive Bjorn, Erling, and Kari to erupt in bursts of bedlam when the hated visits are over. Once, I watch in horror as Erling hoists our cat to the top of the flagpole in a bucket. Sometimes the boys throw rocks at frightened ducks that flap and plunge in a nearby pond, and on one occasion kills one while Kari and Kirsten scream for them to stop. They steal Onkel Ander's hand-rolled contraband cigarettes and smoke behind locked doors. I can smell the acrid smoke seeping under the door. Tante Dagny clenches her fists and pounds the table for order. In desperation she demands immediate, unquestioning obedience and promises a particular kind of violence if she doesn't get it. Kirsten and Kari ally themselves with Tante Dagny, doing their part as women of the house to enforce the law. The boys skulk and murmur retribution. "I'll fix you," I hear Erling threaten Kirsten under his breath.

The crisis alert becomes a fixed state of mind. Air-raid sirens and sudden blackouts send us scrambling down to the cellar at all hours of the day and night. Mundane moments—eating, cleaning up, doing laundry, hiding food—stretch into days of tense waiting, of listening to the hushed whisperings of grownups and radio briefings. While Kari and Erling, with the help of Kirsten and Bjørn, sullenly learn to submit their wills to the militant authority Tante Dagny imposes, I am learning, by observation, not to exercise mine at all.

When the worst of the open combat in the streets is over and the country has been forced into brooding submission, the resistance becomes an unseen but formidable underground power. The characteristic cool Norwegian reticence deepens under a quiet guise of normalcy.

Tante Dagny sets the long table in the dining room for eight. Kirsten and Kari have made a centerpiece of small pine boughs and laid silverware on white linen. Matching napkins encircled by gleaming silver rings lie by each plate. The black curtains are open, letting in the thin remaining light of a late November dusk. It is not quite three in the afternoon. Kari lights a few small candles in silver holders, and I watch as the little flames flare up and cast soft, flickering shadows around the room.

Uncle Anders ushers a tall, important-looking man to the head of the table to my left. He introduces him with mock formality to me as *my father*, and a ripple of laughter erupts from my cousins. I am five now and don't see anything funny. Tante Dagny shoots them a hard look. I sit on several large books on a grown-up chair, dressed in my best clothes.

The excitement in the air is carefully subdued. Dinner—the usual boiled potatoes and fish—is served around in warm bowls. I notice my father, of whom I feel intensely afraid, eyeing me appraisingly from time to time. His demeanor is stern, but not entirely unsmiling. Not, that is, until I nod at Tante Dagny to please, might I have some pickles, which lay glistening in their fragrant juice in a crystal dish just beyond my reach.

My father's face stiffens and he moves the bowl away from me. "No," he says firmly. Murmurs from the grown-ups at the table follow as the impact of his first words to me slowly sink into my bewildered mind. "No," he repeats, looking steadily at me. "You may not have pickles yet."

Apparently a rare commodity, they are reserved for the grown-ups. I slouch down in my chair, shamed by the reprimand of this stranger.

When he departs that night, with no more than a nod to me and a handshake for the others, he carries two large suitcases. I don't see my father again until many months later on the other side of the world.

A few weeks later Tante Dagny and Kirsten begin lining the floors upstairs and down with pieces of luggage. Everywhere I go I am waist high in them, colorful round stickers on both sides, important-looking tags hanging in profusion from their handles. A paper Norwegian flag, with its red background under a blue-and-white cross, dangles in miniature along with the evil-looking swastika.

A sense of somber urgency pervades every hour. Onkel Anders and Tante Dagny hold conferences in low voices by candlelight over dinner. At morning light the grown-ups, which now includes Kirsten, bend over their scanty breakfasts and rehearse the plans and schedules spread out on the table before them.

One afternoon Kirsten hands me a large packet and stands back smiling while I tear it open. In my excitement I barely hear the chatter about the source of my new clothes: a welcome surprise from a neighbor lady who has secret connections in Sweden. I love the plaid wool skirt that has straps that cross in back.

"There's something more in there," Tante Dagny urges.

I dig and find a little white blouse with tiny lace around its collar, and a vanilla-colored wool jacket with small pom-poms on the ties and silver clasps down the front. Tante Dagny, tears in her eyes, gives me a soft brown teddy bear and a picture.

The picture takes my breath away. It is small—I can put it in my pocket. A tall white-and-pink lady angel hovers in the air looking down over two little children crossing a bridge in a storm, a star over her left shoulder. Tante Dagny says I am to keep it with me always, to put it under my pillow whenever I sleep.

In the spring of 1942 it is time for Kirsten, Erling, and me to leave for the United States. Many times we wait at gloomy train stations for documents and passports to be approved, returning frustrated and exhausted to the gray house on the wooded hill. It makes Kirsten cry. We stay at the darkened house a few days more and then set off again, usually in the middle of the night. When Kirsten's and Erling's American status is finally confirmed by the Norwegian government, the American Red Cross intervenes and sponsors our departure. I watch as a white tag bearing the bright red cross is added to our luggage. A chorus of cheers rises from well-wishers at the customs office as the final documents are approved. On a foggy Monday morning we are packed onto a tram under the watchful eye of Nazi soldiers.

Tearfully we wave good-bye to Dagny and Anders, to Oslo, and to all of Norway.

As we speed day and night by train through Sweden and Germany, Spain and Portugal, I miss the many little dramas going on because mainly I sleep. But when the train churns to a stop at a station near a beautiful green park in Lisbon, Kirsten's eyes light up and she jostles me awake. The conductor announces there would be a half-hour stop while passengers get off and others board.

"Let's go!" she cries, happy for a chance to stretch her legs and feel the sunshine. Great flowering trees spread overhead, and the summer heat is lifted a little by a small breeze. We run around crazily, plunging our eager lips into elegant drinking fountains, laughing for the first time in weeks. We chase each other and fall in squealing heaps on the soft grass.

Suddenly Kirsten freezes. A group of Nazi soldiers are coming straight for us. The crowds milling about in the park have thinned, and we are isolated except for the approaching Germans. Grabbing Erling with one hand and me with the other, Kirsten drags us, running and tripping, through the south side of the park, back to the train station, where it is nearly ready to pull out. We clamber aboard in a frenzy, knocking knees and elbows against each other as if trying to board as one body. Kirsten cries softly as we fall into our seats, then throws her head back. I watch her anxiously as tears and sweat flow down her face. Some unnamed terror has passed, but it clings to her for the remainder of the trip. She holds on to us ferociously. The imprint of her fingers on my arm leaves hot red splotches.

That afternoon Erling takes up smoking on the train and becomes more cocky and restless than ever, and for some reason is newly resistant to our sister's sharp authority. He is just fourteen, bright eyed and rosy, but I see a change in his expression. His jaw is set, his look wary.

I watch Kirsten's eyes follow him, her face anxious.

Our journey through Europe takes two weeks, starting out of Oslo, through Sweden, on to Portugal's port city, Lisbon. There we scale the dizzying heights of a great white mountain of a ship, the *S.S. Drottningholm*. Kirsten pulls me from above and Erling pushes from below while I scream and cling, grasping the rungs of the steep ladder to the top deck where I am sure I will fall into the sea below. At last the ship eases into the gray, tempestuous Atlantic, and soon I enter an eternity of seasickness and perpetually getting lost while looking for a bathroom.

One week later the New York harbor welcomes everyone on board as heroes.

From there I see only switchyards and trains. Over and over we push our way on, stumble our way off, wait, sit on our bags, sometimes sleep on them until the next train rolls in and we have to shake ourselves awake in a rush to get on board. Slowly our new train chugs away from the station. Once again I settle down low on the hard seat to watch the telephone poles slide by, wondering at the way the lines dip and rise, sometimes closing in near the window, then shooting off into the distance, but always up and down, up and down.

I have paper to draw with, and with my pencil I try to get the right shape of the swastika. It is hard; I often draw it backward. I fill up sheet after sheet of those ugly symbols. When I get it right I am quite pleased with myself and progress to drawing ladies' faces. My sister's pale face is pretty, but so weary she looks old to me. Her usually soft mouth is set in a hard line, her eyes squint against the light that flashes through the train windows. She is always scanning the crowds.

"What are you looking for?" I ask.

"German soldiers," she answers. Erling is taking off somewhere. "Where is he going, Kirsten?" I ask.

"Trying to find more cigarettes, I guess," she says with a sigh.

Kirsten writes in her diary a lot. When she isn't writing she is soothing me with words like "Everything is going to be all right, Karin. It's really going to be all right."

My father was already in Los Angeles when we arrive; he had gone before us by over six months.

Years later, when I pressed him for information, he reluctantly explained how the physical hardship of fetching enough milk for a schoolhouse full of hungry children the year before had injured his back. He landed in the hospital in Oslo, where the Korda brothers found him and began secret arrangements for getting him out of Norway. They wheeled him down the darkened corridors of the hospital at midnight and brought him to Onkel Anders's house in terrible but stoic pain. After Dad's farewell dinner with us, the Korda brothers met him in a hotel in Oslo and drove him into Sweden, skillfully bypassing checkpoints in the pitch darkness of the winter night. In the morning he boarded a train bound for Japan via Siberia.

I was nearly grown up when Dad finally revealed the hellish details of that journey, and he needed several drinks to begin. Listening to him, I came under the shocking power of his understated images: of unbearable cold in a train crammed with Russian dissidents. Of people struggling aboard, layered in all the clothing they owned. Of getting deadly ill on the vast amount of vodka offered in place of drinking water. Of the endless miles across white, frozen tundra punctuated only by the political prisoners thrown off the train to die in the snow as the train pulled away. Of passing trains splitting the fog with fumes of ether coming from the caboose.

"Why ether?" I dared to ask.

"Passengers were gulping it to stay anesthetized against the cold," he replied.

Dad picks us up from the train station in his 1938 Ford, and drives us to the tiny apartment he has found in Westwood Village. I have the same sensations in the car as in an elevator. My stomach rises and falls, and my head is dizzy. Kirsten lifts me out and carries me into the bedroom, the ceiling light so bright it hurts my eyes.

"Here is your new bed, Karin," Daddy says brightly.

I look at it doubtfully and his smile flickers. I have never slept in a real bed of my own, one without sides. It is so high Kirsten has to hoist me up into it, and I whimper in fear that I will fall out. My father says a brief good night in Norwegian and turns to leave the room. His face is drawn and pale, eyes red with fatigue and stifled emotion. I look away from him, clutch my American pillow and put my picture of the angel underneath it.

We make headlines on the front page of the *Los Angeles Times* the following day: *"Norwegian Girl Keeps War Secrets in Diary."* (I'm told later that is an outright lie.) A big picture accompanies the story. The man I'd seen so seldom, and was to call *Daddy*, is grinning into the cameras poised by the train station, while Erling and Kirsten lean into him with tired smiles. I stand below, frowning, frightened; very grumpy looking for all the celebration going on.

I wake up to a whole new life, every aspect of which needs daily translating.

My father remains peculiarly silent. My five year old presence seems to baffle him. He seems so old to me, though he isn't much past forty. His life becomes a rigid and predictable routine: he leaves for work before I am up, comes home (I anticipate him with a mixture of awe and dread), eats a silent meal, moves to his sitting chair with a cup of coffee and a cigarette, listens to the radio with its droning war news, and then, from that chair, bids me a brief, unsmiling goodnight.

A new day begins: he leaves in the morning before I am up, and I am glad.

Becoming a motherless family of four ensconced in a small Los Angeles duplex in1942 feels like walls closing in. We have traded the mountains and fjords and Norway's high northern sky for the trim streets and close, small dwellings of residential West Los Angeles. The family—uncles and aunts and grandparents and nieces and nephews dotted all over the Norwegian landscape from south to northernmost—is now reduced to just us four, all, with the exception of me, with generations of history here and there. Did Kirsten and Erling really live their early childhood right around the corner in Beverly Hills? Had Kirsten actually gone to school in Los Angeles *and* Norway? Had there ever been, truly, a mother and father, husband and wife, with their two children—Erling and Kirsten—going on outings, picnics, fishing trips, and shopping sprees? No straining of my imagination helps me envision their lives before mother was gone. None of that matters to anyone, it seems; only that we are back where my father has never wanted to be again, and to set the teeth in the living and doing of it. Though he is still a film set designer, Hollywood's 20th Century Fox Studios are a world away from all that was familiar in London and Norway.

He brings home an orange kitten, and I fall in love with the adorable, tiny ball of fur. I experience delight. I giggle and laugh as it pounces in and out of Kirsten's balls of knitting yarn.

But one morning my father runs over it in the driveway on his way to work. I am maddened with fresh grief and weep angrily. Is everything now always to be a taken away?

Alexander and Vincent Korda, the men who secreted my father out of Norway and established him in Hollywood, maintain homes both in London and California. When they are in town they always come to see him and he lights up at their arrival. I can see these men help to ease Dad's misery in his position as an exile, which is how he often describes himself.

"We have an invitation to extend," Vincent announces. My father has me call him Uncle Vincent. He is wearing a dark pin-striped suit and peculiar looking black and white-tipped shoes called *spats*, and holds a cigar loosely in his hand as he speaks. "My son Michael's birthday is coming up." He glances at me and smiles broadly, "Everyone is invited to the party. Dress up. We will feast and celebrate."

The corner of Wilshire and Santa Monica Boulevard, with its beautiful fountain that sends up geysers of water in alternating jewel-lit colors, from palest gold, to amethyst, to garnet, is about to become a treasured landmark—a sign, after some downtown visit, that we will soon be home, but also a reminder of my first foray into the world of the Beverly Hills Hotel, and of Michael Korda, who plays the violin for me as only a true-born Hungarian boy can.

Dad and Erling wear new suits. They take my breath away, they both look so handsome; they seem to think so too. Kirsten and I drag our beautiful Norwegian costumes out of the trunk, and after a careful washing and ironing, we dress each other up. Hers is a black, low-cut embroidered jumper, fitted at the bodice with silver buttons down the front, worn over an embroidered white blouse that is softly shirred around her neck. Mine is a doll size replica of hers in red.

The hotel dining room is softly lit by crystal chandeliers, the table covered with white linen, silvery and gleaming with candlelight. There seem to be a hundred people milling around, gradually being ceremoniously seated by solemn looking men in black suits. The chair I'm given is so low Kirsten runs to find books (phone books, maybe?) for me to sit on, but she is stopped in her tracks by a handsome young man with a towel over his arm. Instead of books, I get a soft, cobalt blue pillow, with tassels hanging down all around like a feline queen's perch. I only half hear the exuberant voices intoning speeches and toasts to Michael Korda as countless waiters serve course after course, then stand like guards behind each guest. They watch from behind as the food disappears, then lunge like fencing artists to remove and replace empty plates with full ones.

For years in Norway we have lived under food rations that made each bite precious and each plateful to be eaten up, whether we liked it or not. Here are waiters with equally militant orders to refill the plates the minute they are in danger of being empty. Slavishly we eat until our eyes bulge, our chins drop, and our stomachs groan. Eagerly the darting waiters deliver yet another mound of mashed potatoes swimming in butter, garden baby peas with mint, and freshly sliced chateaubriand in wine sauce. The room becomes indistinct and the sounds of laughter and clinking glasses fade to a drone. Before we know it, we are being ushered with somber decorum toward one of the private guest cabins behind the hotel, propelled carefully and quickly through the gardens and across the lawn, where we are free to be sick for the duration without disrupting the celebration.

Kirsten and Erling are milling about in our apartment kitchen one afternoon following our elegant dinner at the Beverly Hills Hotel. Kirsten is dragging a big pot onto the stove.

"Bring out the butter," she calls out. "And a lid—quick!"

I stand gaping in a corner of the room. Kirsten is dancing around at the stove. The lid is too late. Small white bombs explode out of the pan, shoot straight up then rain down in a terrifying shower. I scream. Kirsten laughs and squeals. Erling jumps around with his mouth open, trying to catch the bombs on his tongue. I've never seen or tasted popcorn. But my sister's raucous laughter quickly replaces my fright with cautious delight.

But I can't get past something unspoken. Without paying much attention to me as I scurry around picking up popcorn off the floor, Kirsten and Erling are in a happy frenzy of conversation in an unheard of language. I have never heard them do that before, and it frightens me. What are they giggling and talking about? I understand vaguely that for Kirsten and Erling, the U.S. is native soil, but now I really feel…foreign. Both of them are talking so fast, so mysteriously, and I can't understand a word.

They are reverting to their American ways and conversation. It seems the air is full of secrets. I feel unheard and unseen.

Kindergarten is in a school just a few blocks down the neat, sidewalked street. Kirsten walks quietly beside me in the morning and arrives at noon to walk me home. She tries to talk to me, but I walk with my head down, watching the lines on the sidewalk. With my new shoes I kick at the leaves and twigs on the ground. I don't have anything to say. In the classroom with so many children talking at once, laughing, yelling, the swirl of the unknown language engulfs me and I try to shut my ears to it. I am bewildered and sit, wide-eyed and apprehensive.

Weeks turn into months. A cloak of misery lays heavy around me, and I retreat behind it, watching the strange sights and voice sounds around me but perceiving nothing.

My teacher is standing at our door.

"May I please come in and speak to you about Karin?" she asks.

She is dressed in a brown suit and matching hat. The cool air of an early spring night edges into the apartment, and my father says, "Please, come in," in his formal way. He signals for Kirsten to make coffee, and she hurries out to the kitchen.

"I'm so sorry to bother you with this, Mr. Waller," Miss Thorpe says as she removes her hat and sits down on the sofa. "Karin is simply not learning English—at all. She's sitting in a corner as still as a mouse every day as though in a fog."

Kirsten places the cups and saucers on the table with a tray of cream and sugar and our best silver spoons. She goes back into the kitchen and brings a plate of pound cake, carefully sliced and arranged in a swirl. She looks puzzled and throws me an anxious glance.

"I know this is a serious decision for you. But I'm afraid the only way she's going to learn it is if you stop speaking Norwegian to her altogether, starting right away. It's been too many months. She has to begin the transition to her new country—or I'm afraid she's going to have some severe learning disabilities."

Kirsten eyes Dad and Miss Thorpes sadly, but before Kirsten can say anything, Dad quickly agrees. "Of course," he says. "Whatever is necessary."

The next day Kirsten explains what I was listening to without comprehension the evening before. Norwegian—every word!—will be disapproved, disallowed, disciplined out of me. Starting today, it will be cut out with a fierceness as if its sudden, inexplicable *wrongness* is more than equal to the sudden *rightness* of American.

As I forget, and spill out words and sentences from my childhood understanding, I am instantly corrected, new words replaced and stuffed down my throat until I feel like choking. They are drilled into me over breakfast, lunch, and dinner, at playtime with my new friend, Sophia, who lives next door. Kirsten and Theo, Sophia's mother, conspire to enforce the hated transition. Even while I whine in fits of frustration, Theo and Kirsten bend double with peals of laughter over my strange accent and my many amusing mistakes. I hate them. I turn my anger on Sophia with every new English word in my arsenal.

I am often invited to spend the night at Sophia's next door apartment. Her father is warm and affectionate, his broad, brown Greek face always smiling and chuckling. I sometimes hear him singing Greek songs in a lusty baritone through open windows across the driveway. He proudly shows off his beautiful paintings and photographs to me, speaking in English with an accent of his own, and sometimes lets me watch as he tools gold leaf onto leather-covered furniture from his makeshift shop in the living room. It is his trade.

I grow to love Sophia and her father, Sekuris M. Sekuris, who has the strangest name I've ever heard. But I live in mortal fear of tall, slender Theo, whose elegant courtesy seems only a mask which, when whipped off, reveals an ever-ready expression of disapproval. Theo's strict, sharp tone frightens me sometimes. She spends hours fighting with Sophia to finish the food on her plate. Sophia is very picky.

"Do you want to spend the night with Sophia tonight?" Kirsten asks one Saturday afternoon. She is speaking only in English to me now, and waits a long time before forced to translate. Her unyielding discipline is working.

"Yes!" I answer, excitedly at first. Then, as I think it over, "Well, no—oh, I don't know!"

Kirsten gives me an exasperated look. She says she likes Theo and her down-to-earth, no nonsense personality. I notice she spends many afternoons in Theo's tiny dining room over coffee where they talk endlessly, and when Sophia and I burst in they send us right back out to roller skate or play hop scotch on the smooth sidewalks between our apartments.

I decide to spend the night. Leading me into bed after another argumentative dinner over Sophia's untouched food, Theo says firmly, "No getting up now that you're in bed, Karin. If you need to go to the bathroom, don't flush the toilet."

Don't flush the toilet. Clearly this is important, but I can't understand why. In my anxiety to please her I am so confused I can't remember whether to flush or not to flush. She tucks the sheets and blankets under the mattress so tightly I couldn't have gotten up if I'd wanted to.

I lie there stiffly, as immobile as a papoose, and begin to sweat. Would it be all right to call out that I'm too hot? No, I'd better not. I don't dare move or call out to her. I begin to itch. Do I dare pull the blankets loose? I'm afraid she'll get mad. Perspiration rolls down my face. I turn my head to see if Sophia is asleep. She is.

Tears mix with the sweat on my face, and I cry hot, futile tears. I must not awaken anyone. Why is everything so hard to understand? So hard to perform? What are these strange new rules all about?

Somewhere in the course of these suffocating overnight visits, I learn, deep inside where it resides without a conscious murmur, to be glad *not* to have a mother.

Gradually the life we've left fades into a dim memory. Faces and names become fiction to me. I don't cry when I am told Tante Ellen has died of heart failure shortly after we left, although tears stream down Kirsten's face. She had walked with me up the hill to a coffee shop and ordered me a sandwich before breaking the news. "She was your nurse, you know, from when you were born until the war." She searches my face for some evidence of memory—or of feeling. "She loved you so much," she presses on. "It broke her heart when she lost you."

I hear all the words Kirsten says and feel sorry and worried that she is now crying without restraint. But there's nothing inside me about this sorrow. I don't remember anything about Tante Ellen.

We walk home, and I rush outside to play with Sophia, bracing myself for another squabble between us—we who are now two six year-old *American* girls.

3

Displaced Persons

At the close of World War II in Europe and the end of the Nazi occupation in Norway, Kirsten writes to the Høiesen family—Anders, Dagny, their children Bjørn and Kari—a letter of joyful celebration accompanied by all the news of our travels, which up until now could not be sent. The letter was recovered out of Anders' family papers decades later and sent to Erling, who painstakingly translated it word for word, complete with Kirsten's characteristic punctuation.

---

24 June, 1945

Dear Aunt Dagny, Uncle Anders—Kari and "Bönne"!

Can you imagine the jubilation here yesterday when the letter came! The first news for three years—and just while we thought of you and wondered how everything has been with you—with food and clothes and everything else—. Rumors and news come out and one knows not what is fact and what is exaggeration about the conditions at home! But now it is all over—and it must be wonderful again to be able to read and write and discuss freely—to be free from the heavy restriction that sort of subdues one. And we have followed along these past months—We delighted with you over the crown-prince—the King and the government coming home. We saw a news film from the celebration in Oslo—and jubilation was like nothing else. We looked for familiar faces in vain—but just thought that the unrestrained happiness and all the flags and national costumes was overwhelming!...And it wasn't fair because both Father and I wished to be among that crowd of people—!—

It is good to hear that all of you are healthy and fine—and that you also are beginning to get some food—genuine things—!—Kari looks as when we saw her last—(same rascal!)—and Bjørn has certainly become a big boy—both are certainly big now compared to three years ago...How has it been with the schools and lessons?—and teachers?

There is so much to tell that I know not where I shall begin. First and fore-most—"excuse the language" as it was said in the old days. The Norwegian goes in the can when not having more practice than what I have had these years. It is certainly mostly slang expressions that hang on.

We arrived in Los Angeles just four weeks after having left Oslo. The trip went smoothly—we were 72 on the train, and by the time we arrived in Berlin we were like a big family and all the people helped each other and we had it fine—Karin was as good as gold the whole time—and at night she could stretch herself out on the seat—otherwise we others sat and slept the 6 nights; it was not so bad—We were so excited and wide-eyed about everything new that we saw and experienced that there were few that were inclined to sleep!

With the exception of 1 ½ days waiting at the Spanish border we were on the train the whole time—and even there in Hendaye we got to go out on the plat-form only with German guards—and at nighttime they walked under our win-dows—equipped to the teeth with hand grenades and rifles and such—Here at the border two spies were exchanged we came to know later. The Germans got their Johanne Hoffman back and the Americans got Etta Shiber—who had been a German prisoner in Paris after having worked for long—undiscovered—with the underground activity. We stayed one week in Lisbon—got washed really good—(after one week on the train without water). We slept and ate and stood in queue at the Consulate and looked about in the colorful city—. Then we went on the ship—and one week later we were in New York after a delightful boat trip with lots of fun. We three had two bunks and Karin and I slept in the lower one and Erling up in the other. Karin and Erling became seasick the first day—but that wasn't so bad. The worst was when Erling became sick one night he spent up in the overhead baggage-net on the train! (On a train without water, pans and rags too!—Oh my gosh!

But in any case we arrived in N.Y. without anything more serious…but were held onboard the ship one week—with examination by the F.B.I. which was on search for spies and doubtful persons—. Their efforts were rewarded—they caught a fat German with all kinds of funny stuff smuggled away in the shoe-soles and buttons and such! Later he was hung! The Red Cross took us on when we came on land—and arranged transportation from N.Y. to L.A.—We were three days and two nights on that trip—and 2 o'clock at night on the 11th of July we were there—. Father had waited at the station for many hours—and friends of his were there with him when we three came off the train—, tired, but glad! Karin, poor thing, was surely the one that was most confused—. And think—there were photographers and the press and reception and such—! Some pomp for us Waller children! Father was very relieved that we finally were there—and it was good to see him again. He had rented a furnished apartment out in Westwood—(which is not so far from where we lived before)—and little by little we fell in with the day-to-day living again—but the first days it was mostly resting and eating—Also there was a steady stream of Norwegians—none we knew—who came by in order to hear about how every-thing was in Norway—and we told about everything we knew to tell—and many had family at home—also—would very much like to know if we knew Olsen and Pettersen and Hanse—in Drobak, Lillehammer and Moss! There was entertainment from radio and film—and much fun.—So it was to come into household activities—rationing, food, shopping and such—and with some practice and with much thinking back to what I learned in the kitchen at your home and at the school kitchen I got myself into it without too much difficulty and burned food!—After a while we ventured out and became acquainted with the neighbors—and Karin found herself a playmate at the house next to us—and you know Karin chatted away in Norwegian and the other went on in American and neither of them understood but they played with each other's dolls and had lots of fun together...

That fall Karin went into kindergarten—and Erling to school right across the street from us.—Karin understood very little of what was going on...Erling got himself right away a number of pals who were all very impressed at having a genuine "refugee" in their circle! He had it a little difficult, also, to begin with, with the language and new instruction-methods and subjects—but it went—. I began an evening course in business subjects—and during the day took care of the house, gossiped with the neighbors and exchanged recipes!

One year later an English lady came out here with her son from England (we knew them from before)—and she sought a job—and a place to live. It hap-pened that Father bought a house and they came and lived with us and she took over the house and I got a job at the library at the studio where Father is.—He works now at Fox which is only 10 minutes from home by car—. Karin changed schools—to one nearer the new house and Erling continued where he was.—In June this year the son went int the Navy—(one is called up when 18—Erling can almost not wait) and now it is only us four. I am working still—Karin is in third grade—Erling has two years left in "middle-school".

Father works every free minute he has in our garden and it is really pretty now.—We have a small lawn in front of the house with flower beds by the door—and oranges close by the street—and some trees here and there (lovely to describe—that one must say—) Also in the back-yard there are trellis works or whatever they are called—and there he has grapes (that first this year will bear fruit.)—and we have vegetable beds with beans and onions, carrots and lettuce and tomatoes—and more—and something like a balcony or veranda on our house faces out towards the back-yard. It is fine there in the evening—we can sit out and have our coffee there—and right now all the flowers are in full bloom—So we have it really fine...None of the furniture is ours—they came with the house—but we hope soon to get a piano. Karin ought to soon take lessons.

This letter is surely nearly a whole book.—

Read that Norway has declared war on Japan—. Have hope that it won't be long before they give up—already now there is talk about peace negotiations—. The war down in the South Pacific has not been easy—very tough, and many lives lost so that now they need to strike the cities on Japan itself. Many say—the military—that it can be 18 months before Japan is defeated—others maintain that it all could be over by Christmas time.

We have not been in danger on this coast.—In 1942 a submarine dared to come in to the coast and they sent in a few torpedoes and damaged a pier and some things.—but nothing more happened.—Early this year some balloons began to float in over California and Oregon—and dropped down. Some curious people went out to investigate and the secret mechanism became loosened by the handling, and the whole thing went to worst—. Many balloons came over—and it is said that they were sent out from Japan.—

Butter, sugar, cheese, meat, and canned food are altogether rationed—and often it is difficult to get hold of these things—but with queue standing and searching, it goes.—We have enough of everything—and right now we are pickling and canning. Gasoline is also rationed—but that hampers no one.

It is surely best to end this letter before it becomes too thick!—

Be so kind to greet everyone—Ellen, Olav and little Gro—Aunt Ingrid's Mirjam and otherwise everyone else we know—Hoping it stands well too with them. Write soon again.—Heartfelt greetings from

Kirsten

Kirsten has begun her night class in business while playing Mama and general disciplinarian during the day. Erling starts high school in the fall. He remains, in my eyes, an ever-lurking mystery, furtive and restless, strangely invisible and unconnected to me. He whistles in the dark, whips in and out of the house as though he always has somewhere to be. Where does he go? I can only sense, in the most primitive way, that Erling will not be contained. His intelligence and curiosity will lead him to explore the world in ways we could never have foreseen.

The small house Kirsten describes to Onkel Anders and Tante Dagny in her letter seems fabulously huge to me. The neighborhood seems palatial, on a street just south of Sunset Boulevard in Brentwood, every house flanked in front and back with beautiful green lawns and big, flowering trees, but no sidewalks. Sadly I leave Sophia and our roller skates behind.

But the price is a bargain: $11,000, furnished right down to the silverware in the kitchen drawers. The couple who owned it have divorced and left everything:

drapes, carpets, tables, chairs, beds. In the following years very little of this bounty is replaced. To me it eventually seems drab and worn, but for my father it seems to have been a comfort following the wreckage of all that had been home to him in Norway before the war. It is as though the idea of permanence, even that which is represented in the furnishing of a house, has evaporated for him forever. He seems only too willing to live with someone else's drapes and carpets. It is good food he is after, and lots of it, meals abounding with good meat and drink, four courses at every dinner, with real butter when we can get it, and an appropriate solemn appreciation from us all. We are not allowed to chatter while eating at that table.

In the spring I begin third grade and try to fit in with the all-American, carefree children of upper class West Los Angeles. Schoolwork is hard; I feel distracted and still always on some vague danger-alert. My English has supplanted Norwegian, but is still expressed uncertainly, accompanied by a lisp and a stammer. But it is arithmetic that makes my stomach ache! To my relief, my father takes no notice as Kirsten works stubbornly to help me overcome the mysteries of subtraction, but I'm a lost cause. My stomach cramps up in knots at the sight of numbers and I resort recklessly to making up answers on my assignments. Any old numbers will do! There is an F beside *arithmetic* on my report card.

Dad puts on an old, limp brown shirt and baggy pants and spends his weekends planting a garden: pole beans and cauliflower and rutabagas. He makes a swing for me out of sturdy rope with a narrow wooden seat, well sanded and varnished, and hangs it under a trellis draped with a lush, blooming trumpet vine. As I swing I dreamily watch the sun flashing and burning behind the leaves above me. I begin to adore my father, though it seems he hardly ever looks me in the eye, and never, ever embraces me.

To say that Dad is cold and unapproachable during these years is not really fair, because soon enough I come to learn that beneath the exterior he is hot with anguish. He is bombarded by the needs of his family, needs he is inadequate to meet in his permanently shell-shocked state. The loss of his wife to that impenetrable "world of her own"; the blame having been laid on him on top of it all—I can see agony etched on his face.

It is from his own mouth, years later, that I learn that he was indeed blamed. But who told me he had dallied with other women, been discovered, and assaulted by Mother's relatives with the force of an outraged army I don't know to this day. Though it is the war that catapults him out of the country, the event conveniently fulfills their determination that he is to stay away from my mother forever. All the feelings engendered by personal failure, betrayal, guilt, and loss of the love of his life has combined to wage an accusation upon his soul from which he can never free himself. He is like a man in prison with his head in his hands, rocking.

The move to Brentwood with its garden to be designed and house to be enlarged gives him a place to work out some of the energy of these torments. His artistic creativity is an outlet straight from heaven. To what he considers the detestable background of Doris Day's singing and Harry James' jazz, he sets himself to the tasks of creating form and beauty, order and function, even while his stomach churns up ulcers. While these burn and chafe, he makes me a doll house, an austere little building wall-papered in each of its three rooms with left-over Christmas wrap. The smallest of these rooms fairly shouts with red poinsettias. In our own house he trains ivy from a strong stalk near the back door to trail indoors along the kitchen ceiling. The green tendrils cooperate perfectly, creating an indoor arbor from the laundry room to above the kitchen sink. Beneath the gently drooping, robustly green ivy Dad places his bar: a seltzer bottle and a tall bottle of Bourbon.

And so it is true that my father felt more deeply than his countenance ever betrayed. My perception of him was simply wrong. But what is also true is that none of us who lived with him could find access to the sweet sap of his caring in ways we craved as children. Touches, hugs, eye-to-eye affirmations were all locked away from us and our frustration knew no bounds.

But…he did make me that doll house, which, being very sparsely furnished, I soon bored of and unthinkingly give away to a neighbor child. It is one of the few times I witness Dad's pent-up wrath. I think he may have even cried—privately, of course.

The antidote to all the suffering he feels—and causes us to experience our share in—is humor. Humor so dry and pungent with irony that we are captivated, undone to the floor with laughter. His talent is to make fun of everyone and everything, dismantling all pretensions from every quarter until there is nothing left but mirth at the sheer *silliness* of—well, everything. On the heels of these rare times of sardonic hilarity he generously rewards us by taking us out to dinner, followed maybe by a funny English movie, often staring Alec Guinnes, at the local arts theater. There he laughs, silent, strangled laughter that nearly breaks his face, eyes squeezed shut while the laughing tears flow. I am relieved when he can breathe again.

Year after year as Christmas seasons approach he makes sure the favored Douglas Fir is in place on—not before—Christmas Eve, and that all the culinary supplies are on hand for as traditional a Norwegian Christmas as Kirsten can assemble. Deep fried cardamom doughnuts, spritz cookies, roast pork with sweet and sour red cabbage, golden flan that unmolds perfectly, dripping with caramel sauce, bordered with real whipped cream…

My love for him chokes me with its hugeness as much as his ulcers choke him. I long to—and dare not—touch him.

Love and hate. Unapproachable, mysterious. Father-god with clay feet, beyond understanding. Love—and confusion—and fury.

Kirsten talks often about wanting to go to college. After four years of part-time jobs and no future in sight, she says that she is feeling pinched and dried up with all this house-mistressing.

"I could go part time, Dad, and still work and take care of Karin and the house." She approaches this with a level reasonableness that is decisive. Dad grimaces.

For weeks she persists during the evening "family time," drawing the yarn out of her knitting bag, flinging the new stitches on the needles with a speed that makes my eyes pop. Finally he growls, "All right, all right, have your own way!" (Does she already sense he would permanently have her as a surrogate homemaker and mother to me, his surprise-child, if she doesn't do this thing *now?*)

Every evening he orders her to leave the dishes and sit down with coffee and pound cake by the radio to listen to the Evening Concert on the radio. Every evening she brings out her knitting—she is always working on some new, complicated ski sweater—and obediently succumbs to the mandate of silence while Dad reads the paper and listens to Beethoven. (Erling has hocked something in exchange for a trumpet and usually manages to escape these solemn assemblies to the garage, where he plays stridently off-tune until the neighbors complain.) Every morning she gets up to scrape the dried up remains of the previous night's dinner on plates hastily stacked the night before, washes them with scalding water, dries and puts them away, then runs to catch a bus to her part-time job at a dentist's office.

What single father can negotiate three growing, restless children in suburbia without looking back with nostalgia at his cosmopolitan past? In 1945 my father's dreams of living in a fine hotel and biting the ends off of Havana cigars at his leisure have gone up in smoke.

By the time I am eight I have learned how expedient it is to be submissive and obedient, even to my classmates and neighborhood kids. I am discouraged from talking too much, so I listen attentively, not just to words being spoken, but to all the nonverbal communication that takes place in a conflicted household. Kirsten still writes in her diary, and when she isn't home I read it, understanding almost nothing but absorbing the tone and cadence of melancholy.

Dad smokes his pipe and stares into the air, and occasionally hints that we will soon go back to Norway "and leave this godforsaken country." Why he feels this way I can't imagine, but it's unnerving to hear this kind of talk. I am baffled to learn that while the United States is zealously pressing forward in favor of Zionism, Dad is outspokenly anti-Semitic. I'm ashamed of him when he spits out the word *kike* under his breath when describing a Jew he knows. My best, most admired friends in school are Jewish and I would have defended them and their Jewishness with my life if I could have raised my voice against his. That would continue throughout all the years to follow as he muttered invectives against the entire race and looked askance at the ones of my friends who entered our door.

Though the past might have been left behind as though it had never been, yet at the most unexpected moments it is raised as a monument to what is true and proud in my father's life—including his pure Scandinavian heritage. Whenever Erling's all-American buddies ("delinquents," as Dad dubbed them) come barging in the door I always fear that Dad will kick them out instead of merely threatening it under his breath. Visitors seem to have to pass some kind of checkpoint before entering; his eyes speak this exclusiveness more clearly than words. His walls against the outside world are building up higher and thicker every day, and God help the cheerfully naïve person who attempts to push past them. Especially any young man who would attempt to court Kirsten.

Will we stay or go? I wonder. Is it all right to make friends, or will I have to leave them? Is this beautiful place we live in, with the flowering acacia tree on the front lawn and the swing in the back really home? How can it be if my father keeps saying things about going back to Norway soon?

"Watch out," Kirsten hisses to Erling while clearing the dinner table, "Dad's planning his escape from exile again." Erling grunts with an unamused half-smile.

It is with huge surprise that we receive the news that Dad has hired a housekeeper.

Mrs. Cornwell is a gray-haired lady whose ample bosom is always corseted and fragrant with small festoons of lavender from her native Scotland. Her hair is scooped up around cotton "rats" that create a soft halo around her plump face, the rest fastened with fine hairpins in a little bun at the crown. When she removes the rats at night and lets her hair down, I hardly recognize her. She occupies one of our three bedrooms, and for a time her son, John, lives with her there. He is a shy, handsome boy of sixteen with black, curly hair and bright blue eyes.

Our family of six seems tightly packed in that house, especially as I compare us to our affluent neighbors who have space to spare with no European exiles on board. I share my room with Kirsten, and my father shares his with Erling. Since Kirsten is thirteen years older than I we don't make very compatible roommates. At night she puts a scarf over her bedside lamp so she can read while I am trying to sleep. Her books include poetry by E.E. Cummings and T.S. Elliot. (Her favorite line: "*This is the way the world ends/this is the way the world ends/this is the way the world ends/not with a bang but a whimper.*" The haunting words make me shudder and I wish the man hadn't written them.) But she most enjoys reading the dictionary.

The light annoys me no end, and I toss fitfully while she studiously ignores me. Sometimes the scarf begins to smoke, creating a large black-rimmed hole. One night it catches on fire and Kirsten jumps up and stomps it out with her bare feet. Her face, to my satisfaction, looks flushed and embarrassed as she crawls back to bed.

During those first years, before and after the war was over, we have ration books, which Kirsten had learned very artfully to manage between the four of us. Now it is Mrs. Cornwell who takes them to the local Safeway for redemption. On Saturdays we walk together down our long, winding street to San Vicente Boulevard, where we catch a bus, pass a golf course and my elementary school, then get off at the market. Mrs. Cornwell takes with her a cloth shopping bag with twine handles. It is cautiously filled, and together we lug it back, trudging resolutely up the long, curving street past houses much more auspicious than ours.

Sometimes we stop at a little shop near the market where she can buy made-to-order cotton underpants for me that don't require elastic, an item in short supply due to the war-time rubber shortage. These pants are baggy, strangely shaped things that she cheerfully calls "knickers." They are uncomfortable and they embarrass me; no one else in our neighborhood has tailor-made knickers.

Mrs. Cornwell cooks and bakes for us, making sure I get four cooked prunes with my oatmeal every morning before school. When she discovers my father likes rice pudding, she serves it at least twice a week. "I wish I'd never mentioned it," Dad mutters with a wry smile, digging once again into the creamy depths beneath the high, perfectly swirled meringue. I am anxious for her should this truth comes out, but if she heard it she doesn't acknowledge it.

Mrs. Cornwell teaches me the mysteries of meringue with frowning concentration. "Never allow the sugar to bead," she warns. "Those droplets you think are so cute are a sign of improper beating."

It is lovely to come home from school to her gentle "Hello, love" and have tea with her at our breakfast nook while she smokes her Pall Mall cigarettes and shows me how to make smoke rings. She asks me about school and lets me talk away about the teachers and the mean kids while she pulls the cellophane wrapper off the pack just so far, then carefully burns a hole in it with the lit end of her cigarette. After filling her round cheeks with smoke, she presses her lips to the hole and slowly blows all the smoke in. With her chubby finger she gently taps the bottom of the wrapper and out comes perfect, lazy, undulating smoke rings. Sitting there with the smoke wafting gently around me, the cups filled with Lipton's Brisk Tea, sugar, and milk, English-style, I relish the contentment, and I giggle.

PART II

Angels of Light

4

Lead Players

Meredeth has come.

She has walked in the front door, arm around Kirsten's waist, and has captured us all.

It is not just her appearance, though that is striking. Her beauty is alive. Her eyes gleam with unspoken promises of good things to come, better than you've ever had before. Her gaze is seductive; before realizing you'd better be cautious, you believe her. She's been in the house for ten minutes and I don't ever want her to leave. When she does, she leaves a turbulent, sparkling wake like a disturbed sea behind her.

From that day she seems resolutely determined that I understand how important I am in the scheme of things. My world cracks open. I am ten, already craving romance. Meredeth reminds me of a thoroughbred mare, with her slender neck and regal head. I know what a Greek goddess is supposed to look like from my father's book on Greek architecture, and she reminds me of one—the mystique of a sculpted female presenting her perfect profile toward the sea in lofty reverie. For her face is sculpted like Venus, with a broad, high forehead delicately embossed with dark, straight brows that arch nearly at the temples.

She and Kirsten have met at UCLA in one of their undergraduate classes, and my painfully shy sister seems to have been drawn to her without a struggle. Every time she visits, she brings gifts. Today she hands me a little book of Bach Minuets.

"You must learn to play some of these for me." She smiles, then pulls a second book out of her purse, drags the dining room chair out to sit in, and writes something on the opening page. She puts it into my hands with a smile. It is a book about Edvard Grieg, the Norwegian composer whom I already know. "Here—I've written you a little note. Will you read what it says?"

"*To my dear Karin,*" I read aloud, "*whose elfin charm is just like Grieg's music. Love, Meredeth.*" She has known me for only a few days—and she says this. But I feel as though she knows me inside out. *Elfin charm*—whatever it is, I want it. With blushed pleasure I sit right down at the piano and begin showing off my sight reading. The sour notes come at once. Meredeth smiles indulgently at me. "Never mind. You'll get it! Isn't his music beautiful?"

Meredeth has come, and our whole world is irreparably altered; an impassible chasm now lies between what was and what is.

Kirsten does not idolize as I do; life so far has built caution and a keen eye for subterfuge in her. It shows in the level way she listens, in the careful pauses before she responds. And yet it is clear she is miserably vulnerable to Meredeth's attentiveness, which focuses on her in an unrelieved manner in the months that follow. Kirsten is a princess in disguise, a Cinderella among the cinders of an austere and lusterless life, needing to be discovered, reborn, re-dressed, and the clock is ticking. I watch, fascinated, as Meredeth devotes herself to this cause with a firm and dedicated hand. Kirsten tries, it seems, to withstand the doses of grandiose accolades Meredeth applies to her modest ego, but I fleetingly remember at times that she, too, is *motherless*. A motherless daughter in need, though her deepest soul would try to deny it.

Meredeth brings out lipstick and mascara.

"Darling, you must smile more!" she purrs. "You have such a beautiful smile!"

In time, a transformation occurs before my dreamy eyes. Meredeth has polished Kirsten's quietly elegant beauty to a deep sheen. She is about to become a shining presence in her new circle of friends, though I can see she never believes it when they tell her.

Next, with an eagerness that borders on religious zeal, she is teaching Kirsten how to cook something other than fish and boiled potatoes, and talks Dad into buying a whole set of Revere Ware for "waterless" cooking.

"Now," I hear her say, "what about your wardrobe?" It is true that Kirsten hasn't bought anything but the basic essentials in clothing for years; something in which to stay warm, something in which to stay cool. J.C. Penney's would do for most of that.

"And Kirsten, you must speak up! You have so much to say, to share with others! Don't play mum! You have more to offer out of that beautiful head of yours than anyone I know…just *relax*."

"How do I relax?" Kirsten moans. "I feel self-conscious, uneducated…and, well, poor compared to—" But Meredeth doesn't let her finish.

"No comparing! You are your own sweet self, and besides that I'm not as rich as I look, it's what you do with what you have." Upon which she promises to bring in a whole barrel full of discarded clothes from her own closet next time she comes over.

I am watching a private charm school. I have no idea I'm next in line, but when the time comes, I will be a very eager apprentice. Kirsten is casting me an uneasy look. Does she already see I have been won? I get the feeling she would prefer I not be present with her new college friends—especially Meredeth—but the die is cast. Wherever they go, I will try to be invited to go along. Soon I am insisting on it, pushy as only a ten-year old can be.

Meredeth knows how to handle that. She makes sure I believe I'm even more cut of her same cloth than Kirsten is, and we form a secret alliance of understanding regarding this premise right in front of Kirsten's eyes. My time with Meredeth will come.

After Meredeth has shown Kirsten how to dress, how to dance, and how to drink, I'm aware by simple observance (and a lot of eavesdropping during their most intimate times of ardent conversation in our room) that she tries to teach her to relax about other things. But I see Kirsten shaking her head *no*. Capturing men is openly Meredeth's prime goal in life, and it is clear that her undeniable success at this is shocking to Kirsten.

"I'm not ready for all that," she protests. Meredeth backs off like a cat seasoned in the art of catching mice. "We'll talk more about this," she promises, and gives me a hug to say goodbye.

"Let's face it," Kirsten mutters glumly to Mrs. Cornwell that day over tea. "Meredeth is loose and proud of it."

Nonetheless, it becomes commonplace for me to wake on a Saturday night to the sounds of Kirsten throwing up after long and heavy partying at Meredeth's house.

5

The Princess, the Ball, the Fairy Tales

The front door opens and a breeze carrying Meredeth's gay voice and pungent perfume blows through the house. She gleams, her eyes dance, and her smile grows wide as Alice's Cheshire cat. She waits for our undivided attention while Dad strolls casually out of his bedroom at the "scent of Meredeth", a term he has coined with less irony than is characteristic of him.

"I'm engaged!" she squeals, tilting back her head as if giving rapturous thanks to the ceiling. "I'm engaged to be married!" Dad responds with a rare grin and offers a congratulations from around the stem of his pipe, which is still firmly clamped between his teeth.

Satisfied that even Dad is duly impressed, she adds, "And you are all coming to an engagement ball!" She gives Dad a sidelong grin. "That means you, too, Hans."

He turns away at once, takes his pipe out, and says emphatically, "No, no, not *me*." The congratulatory smile is gone. I look at him and see something I've never seen before: his face is downcast, and it is *sullen!* I blink, look again, and it is gone. Of course he would not have agreed to go, my father!

Meredeth laughs. She has seen the look. "Your mother must have really had to chase him down," Meredeth murmurs admiringly in the wake of his departure back to his room.(I soon learn "chasing him down" is her standard procedure where romance is concerned.) Then I can almost hear Kirsten thinking, *Other people roll up the rugs and dance, but Meredeth gives balls—and thinks my father is going to attend!*

Kirsten has already visited the massive house where they have recently staged a wedding for a friend, and I can tell afterward that she had fallen under a spell, if not entirely Meredeth's, at least that of the Big House itself. "They simply remove a sliding wall between two rooms," she answered my question about it

44

that evening, "which are really living room and library, and *voila!* A ballroom! Everything is so—*massive.* Even the grand piano looks small in that corner by the French doors. Then there are these fabulous Persian rugs and big oak tables and huge stuffed chairs, and a stone fireplace like something out of a castle. If you push everything against the wall, there's room for a dozen couples to waltz! Or maybe forty!"

"But—how do they do a *wedding?*" I had asked.

"They move everything out, except the piano of course, line up a couple of hundred folding chairs, hang garlands of flowers all over the place, and put big standing candle holders everywhere. I've never seen candles like that. Later they move all that out, slide in a portable bar, and there's your reception!" As I remember Kirsten's description, I longed for the day I could see it too.

Meredeth breaks into my reverie. "You, my dear little Karin, are definitely invited to come, too." Kirsten's face falls.

"Meredeth, I don't think—"

"Oh, no, I insist!" She grins broadly at me, lays two—no, three (is she still hoping for "Hans"?) embossed invitations on the coffee table—and whirls around to leave.

It is settled. If I am allowed to go to the engagement ball, I will stay home and let the wedding be for the grown-ups.

"Who is Meredeth engaged to?" I ask while getting ready for the big night. "Is it someone from U.C.L.A.?"

"She's fallen madly in love with a tall, handsome man from the Dutch East Indies," Kirsten tells me while she brushes her fine, fly-away blond hair. "She met him last year through her father's oil business." There is a mocking tone behind her smile. "It all happened through love letters. Ha! I wonder what she said to him." Kirsten is trying on one outfit after another, all of them landing in a discarded heap on the bed, and she is blushing with frustration.

I revel in how it feels to be putting on stockings for the first time and twist around one way and then another to pull the back seam straight. It is clearly understood that I am to stay strictly in the background and not mingle in any way with the grown-ups.

"In fact," Kirsten says firmly, emerging from the bathroom in a pale blue silk dress so classic it doesn't look five years old, "your best bet is to get upstairs into Meredeth's room while the festivities are going on and find a good book to read."

I am too excited to care what part of the house I am relegated to, so I nod agreeably. I notice while doing so how beautiful, really beautiful, Kirsten looks.

She is so softly blond, like moonlight, and her clean, square features wear a poised mask of serenity under the upswept hairdo. I am happy to see her dressed up, and I love the delicate glitter of the silver jewelry she has pinned at her throat. Though I'm glad she is going to a party, I feel uneasy for her too. I remember the Saturday night sicknesses.

My dress is white, with huge puffed sleeves and eyelet trim around the ruffles at the hem. I feel as gorgeous as one of the stars in my girlfriend Louise's movie magazine.

Kirsten eyes herself critically in the mirror and I catch sight of her hands. They are red and knotty. She sees me staring. "Like a charwoman's," she says unhappily. She shoots a bitter glance at me as I sit quietly on the bed. "I wish I had hands like you. They don't look like they've ever done a lick of work." I look down at mine guiltily, realizing that, compared to hers, they haven't. She pulls off the old ring she has tried on for effect, and the doorbell rings. Meredeth has come to fetch us in her car.

"Oh! You look simply beautiful, Kirsten!" Meredeth exclaims, eyes warm with approval. Kirsten blushes and mumbles something. Meredeth opens the back door of her roadster and offers me her gloved hand, like a prince helping a princess into his carriage.

"Karin, you look so grown up! Now, for heaven's sake, don't go off somewhere. Everyone is dying to meet you. And are we all going to *dance!*"

"Me too?" I ask. "Really?" Kirsten levels a forbidding look at me from over her shoulder.

"Of course, dear, and why not?" Meredeth tucks Kirsten's coat around her. "Isn't that what parties are for?" She beams at Kirsten, "But it's you, darling, who will be the new queen of the ball!"

I gaze out the window in wonder as cars follow us in a processional up the long driveway and park with ease in twos and threes beside us. From where I stand, waiting for Kirsten to get out of the car, Hollywood, Beverly Hills, Westwood, and Brentwood can all be seen in a long, sparkling sweep—and beyond all the lights, the Pacific Ocean, faintly lit with twilight.

As tall, handsome men in black suits, shiny shoes, and boutonnieres escort women out of their cars and call greetings to one another, I am engulfed by a fragrance I have never smelled before. There, flanking the stone walkway leading to an enormous oak door, are gardenia bushes in full bloom, and by the door, a huge basket filled with succulent buds in their prime.

"Kirsten! How lovely to see you," Gisela von Breuner calls. "You are beautiful as only a Norwegian can be. Now pin this on and not even my husband will be able to take his eyes off you." She secures a perfect gardenia right below the silver pin on Kirsten's dress and propels her through the door with a kiss on her cheek. "There are men in there who have been waiting hours to meet you. And Karin, you elfin child, here is a gardenia for each hand. You'll have to put them in your hair when they ask you to dance, won't you?"

Gisela Von Breuner, as stunning in middle age as Meredeth in her twenties, has dark eyes, alternately piercing and warming out of a magnificent sculptured face. Just an older version of Meredeth, I think.

If the house is a setting fit for a princess, Meredeth is its centerpiece. It is around her everything revolves like a spinning garden of delights which, by simple centrifugal force, can't be stopped: the music, the dancing, the laughter. What a bold—outrageously bold—flirt she is. The shyest of men give way and are captivated, eyes glazed with wonder at the ripe promise that is Meredeth, even on this occasion of her engagement. She not only knows this, she insists on it. I could tell this was true the first time she laid eyes on my father.

The fragrance of the gardenias makes me giddy, and to my sister's alarm I run up and down the spiral staircase, peering into bedrooms and dressing rooms, finding mirrors everywhere to admire myself in.

◆   ◆   ◆

Mrs. Cornwell always grimaces and slightly ducks when Meredeth blows in like a whirlwind and shakes the rafters with her effusive, squealed greetings. Today she winces and disappears to the kitchen when Meredeth hugs my father and whirls him around, giving him a wide and challenging grin.

I watch this encounter in horrified fascination, for this is the only time I ever see warmth for a woman fill his eyes, and it scares me. That glazed look; I've seen it before in men younger than he. How mortifying that she is the only human being allowed to touch him when we, his children, are not. But before the thought is complete in my head she turns and advances on me, grabbing me up in a bear hug with a laugh, saying I am the most beautiful young girl she's ever seen.

Mrs. Cornwell, always conscious of her place in our home, remains gracious and detached. She has been busying herself in the kitchen, and now emerges bearing a steak-and-kidney pie with a golden crust made with pure lard, propped up in the center by a shot glass. Meredeth rhapsodizes over her, oohing and aahing and "Will you please give me the recipe?" Mrs. Cornwell's damp, pink face beams at that in spite of herself, and I distinctly hear her saying that perhaps she might, and if it's all right with Mr. Waller, she might stay for dinner and have some with us.

◆   ◆   ◆

My friend Louise and I live in the relatively comfortable pre-adolescent routine that begins each morning by walking the single mile down our lush, carefully landscaped street, then past the local country club and golf course to our school. Her chatter consists mainly of passing judgment on her teachers, most of whom I am to inherit the following semester.

Louise is more than just a playmate; she is often my bank. The inequities of our cultural background show up in our social lives and put unwanted pressures on my father's pocketbook—the frequent movie going, the clothes shopping, excursions to Wil Wright's Ice Cream Shoppe (the most expensive ice cream in town). Louise takes dancing lessons and attends *cotillion*, a word I don't understand. (A dancing school?) Perhaps the post-war prosperity experienced by the families in our neighborhood make these expenses seem small, but to my father they are outrageous indulgences, and, of course, *silly*. My allowance is never enough to meet them, but somehow Louise's always is, for both of us. In spite of the monetary burden she silently assumes, she holds me in mystified respect. I travel with my pencil and memories where she can never go. Though she acknowledges that I am the most gullible, easily cowed person she's ever met, she of the beautiful round yellow-brown eyes and hemp-colored hair accepts me without condition, and I know she, being six months older than I and in a higher grade at school, has committed herself to protecting me.

A fear has begun to accompany our walk back home from school during the years following the end of the war, something our families don't like talking about and explain only briefly. To us it seems as if monsters have been let loose to terrorize us on the streets beyond the school, but they are only men from the Veteran's Administration Hospital a few miles away.

"These are war-torn soldiers, wounded in body and mind, and they have nowhere to go except the local tavern," Louise's mother explains quietly. As if she'd rather not, but knowing she must, she elaborates sadly: at the bar they drink themselves senseless, and then wander the perimeters of the golf course looking for stray golf balls, which, when sold, buy them their next drink.

These red-eyed men make the walk home from school a small nightmare. They seem to look at us menacingly as they lurch along searching for those balls, and I am sure that if we come within a foot of them they will tear us limb from limb. "Uh-oh," Louise is whispering. "Here comes a drunk man." Something warns us that to run will be to invite their chase, so we walk stiff-legged, as frightened children do, not daring to look to the left or the right, clutching our books tightly to our chests and marching ahead as fast as we can without appearing to run.

This looming menace creeps into my bed with me at night. I lie awake, afraid to go to sleep lest I die. Once I fall unwittingly to sleep, I dream evil dreams of eyes staring, a nameless face bearing down on me with a leering smile from which I cannot escape. I awake in terror, stomach aching, limbs shaking. A sleepy, anxious Kirsten holds me tight while the tremors tear through me, and then I throw up. It's over. Then she gathers me, limp and weak, into her own bed and snuggles me close, where we lie like two spoons until I fall asleep again. Such moments of comfort from her patient warmth fill me, cover me, cradle me until I am in a very heaven of peace. We sleep.

Kirsten isn't at home the night the dream repeats itself and awakens me. The nameless face, malignantly staring and smiling, not blinking, eyes boring into my face as if to absorb and annihilate me—and I awaken. I am engulfed by panic. I am sure I'm dying. Wildly I run into the room where Mrs. Cornwell is sitting in her bed reading, her soft gray braid all undone and hanging down her back, her stout, bosomy body oozing from the edges of her nightgown.

"I'm dying, I'm dying!" I scream.

She draws me tightly to her fragrant, lavender-scented breast and breathes a prayer that seems to assert an immediate authority over the black vortex into which I've fallen, and all of it dissipates at once. "You are not dying, indeed!" she declares calmly, and returns me cheerfully to my bed, tucking me in gently and patting my cheek.

I am never again haunted by that dream or its terror. From that hour Mrs. Cornwell is a wonder of grandmotherly love to me, full of certitude and wisdom. She is the safe harbor to which I can always go.

Early in 1947 Dad applies for citizenship, and there is a family celebration the day it is granted. That summer he takes a brief vacation, packs us all up in his Ford and drives us almost non-stop to the Sierras, where he will teach Erling how to fish. Kirsten brings her pencils and drawing paper so she can sketch gnarled, dead trees by the creek. I wake up in a cold tent to the heavenly sounds of rushing water and the smell of damp Aspen trees and coffee simmering over the campfire.

We arrive home after our allotted two weeks and then it's smoothly back to work. My father's skills are so valuable he is always in demand, never out of work except for those short yearly vacations. During the following three decades, he designs sets on a free-lance basis for many of the great classics, including *The Ten Commandments, Rear Window,* and *The Longest Day.* He admits he is doing some films with Alfred Hitchcock, and states bluntly that the man is a "certifiable sadist."

Louise lives across the street, yet calls me on the phone every day after school or on Saturdays. "For godsake, get off the phone!" Dad bellows from the living room. "She lives only twenty yards away from here!"

I squeeze my eyes shut to Dad's roar and strain to listen. "Mother said she'd take us all to Westwood to see the new Elizabeth Taylor movie, *National Velvet,*" Louise is saying. "You want to go?"

Kirsten has, as is routine on that day, enlisted my help in cleaning the house. Mrs. Cornwell cooks, bakes, and shops, but she doesn't clean very well. She's too stout to scrub floors or to use the washboard to wash sheets and towels.

Kirsten is already well into her weekly rounds, one load of wash done, pinned on the line, drying slowly in the gray June mist. She moves through the house in mute fury, alone in a private war against the disorder that overtakes the house during the week at the hands of her irresponsible brother and sister. Her eyes say, *I'll be darned if I'm going to tell Karin what needs doing. It's easier to do it myself.* When I see that look, I make some half-hearted attempts at assisting. When all possible rearrangements of a cluster of jars and bottles on the bathroom counter have been exhausted, I ask, politely and humbly, for movie money. Then I flee. I can feel Kirsten's hard glare on my back as I slam the door behind me.

Since Louise and I go to the movies in Westwood almost every Saturday, much to my sister's displeasure, celebrity faces become as familiar to us as our own. We compare ourselves to them: *If only we had those crystal blue eyes of Jane Powell,* who lives up the street, *or the elegant smile* and *perfect blond hair of Janet Leigh,* who, a couple of years later, lives right next door. (I watch from my living room window as Tony Curtis escorts Miss Leigh on dates, driving her away in a sleek black car with a cheery wave to her parents. My father and sister and I are sometimes invited by them to come over for drinks and hors d'oeuvres, and I learn to love steak tartar on crackers long before I have my first drink.)

Louise and I devour movie magazines with our after-school snacks, surrounded by the stars of the hour—Joan Crawford, Lana Turner, Elizabeth Taylor. They all live in the immediate neighborhood. Soon these characters became very old hat—or at least we like, in our adolescent pride, to think so. But the mystique of the film industry is dulled for me because my father works within its walls and hates it. The glamour, the hype, the Hollywood mentality is beneath his dignity as an architect trained in Europe to build houses. He makes his disdain known every chance he gets.

Kirsten, with her Nordic blonde beauty, is approached by Twentieth Century Fox during her sophomore year at UCLA for a screen test. Ignoring Dad's objections, she goes through with it—and passes! They tell her she's beautiful from every angle! Of course, it would mean fixing her teeth and masking her with makeup...Dad's hand shoots up in a wild wave of impatience and he roars, "No daughter of mine is going to get mixed up in this business!" That is the end of it. If she is disappointed she never shows it, although she tells me wistfully after getting into bed that having her teeth straightened would have been nice. She rarely smiles except behind her hand. (Meredeth tries to break her of the habit, but in that she fails.)

The only time he departs from his wordless gloom over his work is a few years later, an event so uncharacteristic I will always think of it as separated and set apart from the time sequence of his dour work life. Would I like to go with him to the studio, have a look at the sets he's designing for "Guys and Dolls"? I stammer, "S-sure!"

"All right," he says, "Be ready at six tomorrow morning."

His eyes gleam and a half-smile pulls at the corners of his mouth as he parks our 1950 Mercury in the back lot of the studio. "Impressed?" he smirks as we cross the huge parking lot full of long, shiny cars. He seems to feel some genuine mirth over this project, and of having me see it. He shows me the blueprints he has laid out on a vast table in a cavernous, high-ceilinged room. He displays the mock-up of one of the New York intersections he's in charge of replicating: Stop/ No Right Turn/No Left Turn/No U Turns/*NO NOTHING*. I'm thinking the last one was added just for my amusement, and he laughs like a boy when I giggle over it.

That is my one and only meeting with his work. And over time his bitterness over his association with Hollywood, and America in general, deepens as the government's hunt for communists begins to invade every movie studio in Southern California. The McCarthy trials make headlines in papers the world over, and many of my father's colleagues are blacklisted and mercilessly fired. He clenches his teeth over every new revelation that some innocent film maker is most certainly a communist sympathizer. As a Norwegian immigrant, and the product of a socialist government, he may have often been in line to dodge those accusations, but I never know this as fact. He never says.

In the days following Kirsten's screen test, which is never again mentioned, she modestly continues her pursuit of a degree in geography, and takes me with her to summer classes. I become quite puffed up and self-important as I sit with her in the large lecture halls of U.C.L.A., lunching with her friends at the sprawling cafeteria on campus. Her friends include me in outings where I am the only child. I never dream Kirsten is simply bound to me by the responsibility of baby-sitting.

The days of hot summer and cool winter afternoons when Louise and I used to sit on her front steps playing jacks or trading cards with neighbor kids are behind us. Now card games and Monopoly boards are left where they were last dropped in favor of magazines like *Silver Screen* and *Motion Picture*. An occasional *Modern Romance* crops up as well, and we spend whole afternoons sprawled on her bed reading, each in our own world of romance run wild. It makes me think of Meredeth and her love life, and wonder.

The paradoxes in my life make me bone tired. At school I am still the celebrated Norwegian refugee, a novelty and mystery. I never asked for all that kind of attention; it always surprises me, but still I rise to embrace those romantic images of myself. I allow myself to be draped in an aristocratic cloak, though in reality I feel insecure and pinched by nervousness around my classmates. I develop a stubborn stammer in a class I lead as "class president". I drop books on the floor in front of my locker. I start wearing loud pink lipstick.

My father fuels the confusion by declaring that I am becoming too American and scowls at my appearance as he looks me over from top to bottom. "Wipe off that lipstick!" is what he says, but what I hear at school is that I look like a white witch without it.

At home, critical anti-American conversation seeps in to our home like a toxic fume. Whenever Europeans of any stripe—especially, it seems, the Norwegians—gather in our living room, some of whom are long-time residents of Los Angeles and favored visitors, the talk is punctuated with snarls of contempt. Books begin appearing on the coffee table, and the titles make me shrink inside: *The Ugly American; A Nation of Sheep*. I can't understand the conversations surrounding these subjects, but I sense a cynical, sardonic spirit behind the words. The very sound of the Norwegian language revolts me. I flee to my room when the voices rise in high-volume discussions that sound like a dissonant chorus of gibberish to me. I know I won't be missed. Oh, the disgust I feel as I slam my bedroom door against that sound. Yet, I long to be included. Even so, I know I will never be a part of the most vocal expressions coming forth from my own family—on holidays, with guests, every special occasion—for they are always in Norwegian, and I can't understand a word. I am living in two worlds, one with a secret language I am not allowed to know. Secrets. I turn glumly aside in Kirsten's and my room to my solitary pleasures: books, pencils, drawing paper. I mope. The maddening drone of voices of the inner circle outside my room, rising and falling in discordant pitch, dissonant to my ears in that language beyond my comprehension, makes me clench my teeth.

When no one is around after school except Mrs. Cornwell, I learn to play the piano, although my lessons with Mrs. Forschner down the street are torture. She has peculiar bugged-out eyes, a high, strident voice, and a habit of pounding on my hands with her long, bony fingers whenever I make a mistake. I love the romantic, sometimes plaintive music, even the effort of learning its difficult mathematics and techniques, for music has become the language I understand best. But I am hating the painful knots in my stomach as I march down the street beforehand. Her face is scary, and I don't like the way her husband looks at me, somewhere below my neck.

Meredeth is always watching me. She faces me with a determined optimism when I wither in self-doubt. Steadily, she replaces Kirsten and Mrs. Cornwell as the constant in my world. With her all things are possible, it seems. I trust her to have the last word, the best plan, the immediate cheerful answer, because she always does. So then, is there really any other choice but to trust and agree? While an undercurrent of pessimism rules like a creed between my father, my sister, and the world at large, Meredeth brings an insistent, airy lightness wrapped around endless opportunities to celebrate. Intrusive as a hurricane, she makes me flinch and duck when she comes through the door, but I adore her for it and stop mea-suring the guarded responses she evokes in everyone. Joyfully I let her sweep me into her plans, whatever they might be—to spend the night, to spend the week-end, to spend a week or two at the Big House—how about the entire summer? She flirts her way over and around every objection until both Dad and Kirsten smile weakly and relent. Out we go to the zoo, or on long drives to the beach at Malibu, where a famous German friend of hers owns a horse ranch across the highway from the sea and trains thoroughbreds. I am treated as the "special" guest of honor at lunches on her expansive patio while Meredeth introduces me, along with her other friends, to her fiancé. I get to go with them to the Greek Theatre to see *Swan Lake*, the Hollywood Bowl for the Russian *Bolshoi Ballet*, the Little Gypsy restaurant on Sunset Boulevard for Hungarian cuisine.

Kirsten's unease intensifies, and I begin to sense vaguely that in Kirsten's mind Meredeth's largesse brings with it a sense of charity, and something more subtle still that I can't define. I only know I don't like the pained expression on Kirsten's face when Meredeth's name comes up. For Kirsten has retreated from her. She acts suspicious, wary when I receive Meredeth's calls. It is as if she is thinking, but doesn't dare ask, how far will her friend go to change the very fabric of the Waller household? Who has control?

"Meredeth, Meredeth," I hear Kirsten muttering to herself one gloomy winter afternoon while sorting laundry in our bedroom. "How can I say no to her? I owe her so much." She picks up a hand-me-down skirt Meredeth has insisted she take, a soft brown cashmere plaid, and abruptly drops it on a chair. She watches me as I enthusiastically paw through mountains of clothes Meredeth has picked out for me and dumped on my bed, begins to say something, then stops and turns away. But I am getting so irritated at her frowns. I know—and am *glad*—that Kirsten's role in my life has eroded, that she has become a background figure to me as Meredeth takes more responsibility for me upon herself. Of course she is doing it as a favor—Meredeth has explained that to me—to save Kirsten for herself, for her own life apart from me. Why shouldn't she be grateful for the freedom? But Kirsten's face has that perennially lost expression as she walks out of the room.

Even so, my craving for Meredeth's attention has become an unquenchable gnawing even to me. I try to shake it off but can't. I begin to feel a new emotion twisting in me whenever Meredeth talks and laughs with Kirsten. Hadn't she come to take *me* somewhere?

"Kirsten, you've *got* to have some time to yourself!" She has walked in while I'm half-heartedly doing some homework and haranguing Kirsten for help. "Loosen up, dear! You're supposed to be a college student, not Karin's *mother*!" Kirsten blinks her eyes and looks away, then at me. The conflict within can be visibly seen. Probably neither of them knows that I'm smugly aware of it, counting on it, glad of it.

"Look, let me take Karin with me. She can spend the whole weekend at the Big House." Oh, please! I think. "Mother can watch her when we go out with the crowd on Saturday, and Henk would be so glad to have *you* with us this time—but first—we've *got* to get you a new dress."

I droop. Being at the Big House is great, but I'm not so excited about being foisted off on Meredeth's mother.

The wedding staged there one month later is as enormous as any held in a church, but without the clerics. That suits Meredeth perfectly. The couple go on an eight week honeymoon to New Zealand, and Meredeth comes back pregnant. For several months we rarely see her, and life begins once again to take on our own peculiar austere characteristics, unaffected by the Meredeth influence. What a vacuum she leaves in my life! How to go back to where I was before her, with family, with friends?

◆   ◆   ◆

The people closest to us—Theo, Sekuris the Greek, and their daughter, Sophia—have remained close enough since our move for Saturday night poker games at our house. Our next-door neighbors, Bill and Helena, have joined in. Mrs. Cornwell avoids the poker games, but often has afternoon tea with Helena. They all know Meredeth by now, especially Helena, since her son is also a U.C.L.A. student and often joins the crowd that revolves around Meredeth. I once overhear Helena say that she practices telepathy with her, and is highly successful.

While Sophia and I horse around the house and listen to the raucous outbursts coming from the card table, the conversation suddenly becomes subdued, and I say "Ssh!" to Sophia and hold my breath to eavesdrop. What *do* my father and sister say in low tones in English when they have no Norwegians to gossip with?

Theo and Sekuris are talking about Meredeth. I feel the blood rise to my face in anger as they voice their hushed, intimate opinions about Meredeth's influence on all of us.

"She mesmerizes people," Theo is asserting, "She dominates and manipulates them." Theo never was one to hide her ideas about things.

"Especially Karin," Kirsten says.

After some loud laughter from Sekuris (about what? I can't hear—) and some undistinguishable mutterings from my father, the men become unusually silent. Helena begins to add something, but I turn away. Even if it is an argument in Meredeth's favor, I don't want to hear any more.

◆   ◆   ◆

"Come upstairs and see my new baby," Meredeth says. "She's sleeping."

I kneel by Karla Ingrid's bassinet and stare at her. So beautiful—and I realize with a jolt I've never seen a baby before. The same creamy olive skin as Meredeth's, blushed pink on round, downy cheeks, with deep brown eyes and white-blond hair bright as the morning sun. Henk slips in the door behind me and smiles as he watches me adore his daughter. He is long-limbed and lithe, tan as a coffee bean, and blond, with blue eyes that sparkle like a tropical sea. Karla Ingrid has inherited the best of both worlds, it seems.

The new family stays often in the Big House, throwing parties nearly every weekend. I am always invited. But sometimes Kirsten's firm "No!" is law, and I sulk.

And yet, inexorably, Meredeth's world becomes the very fulcrum of mine and Louise stops coming over as much, though I hardly notice. Just as inexorably, the disapproval building around my preoccupation with her masses like an army on the move; it's no longer hidden behind playing cards. Louise doesn't like her and says so. Neither does Sophia. Heated rehearsals of all the reasons I should melt back into the world I was in before she came swirl at me; it is as if Meredeth has become a moral issue. But no one can seem to give me a clear reason, no one can seem to resist Meredeth's sunny intrusions when they are face to face with her. It is as though, when with her, they forget what they've been thinking and saying; all resistance, all objections swallowed by some mental fog. Kirsten grumbles that I am too young to be involved in "that crowd"—which is *her* crowd—but can't say no when Meredeth insists that I come along.

Opinions are murmured between the Sekurises and Mrs. Cornwell, Kirsten and Dad. Meredeth is, in some mysterious way they won't specify, dangerous. One has to be on one's guard with people like her, not to be taken in.

But put them all together with her in one room, and they all are as dazzled as they accuse me of being!

I see the conflict, the hypocrisy, and I want to scream. Meredeth has brought books and clothes and gaily planned delights into my life; things my own family never would do—beach trips, museums, concerts. Taken in? Brought out is more like it! Rescued from oblivion! Neither my sister nor Theo nor Mrs. Cornwell can influence me otherwise.

Anyway, if I am being taken in somehow I *want* to be taken in—taken as far as Meredeth will lead me. I listen, I watch, I adore and emulate. She is alive with the love of life and love, while my sister, my poor sister, is cautious and reticent about—well, everything. No, not everything. She goes away on skiing trips, looking rosy cheeked and excited as she waxes her skis. She goes hiking, runs on the beach, paints beautiful, fragile looking flowers in watercolors. All of it happens somewhere where I am not. I don't have any skis, she reminds me when I wonder why I'm to be left behind. Skis are expensive. And all the rest of the gear! So I see the photos afterward. It occurs to me as I look at a glossy picture of her, snow flying off the tips of her skis: I haven't seen snow since we left Norway.

I reach out, and it is Meredeth who takes me by the hand. In secret conclaves upstairs in their suite she shares her very different, worldly knowledge with me. Intimately, authoritatively, like a teacher to a willing pupil.

She gives me books.

She brings out a ouija board.

6

Angels of Different Lights

The Chinese Elms on Medio Drive look parched in the late summer afternoon heat as I swing my bicycle (courtesy Meredeth) into our driveway. Louise and I have just ridden to Pacific Ocean Park and back, about a five mile trip, and we say a breathless goodbye as she wheels around down the street to her own house. The sea was glorious in its summer blue, and my legs have become strong.

Two years have passed since Meredeth announced that she was going to leave Henk and was filing for a divorce. She felt Henk was unreasonably severe with their daughter. No one seems very surprised that Meredeth is back in town, alone.

Quickly I change into a red cotton skirt and push my feet into sandals. Mrs. Cornwell retreats quickly as Meredeth blows in to whisk me off to the Big House over the Labor Day weekend, and her face says her worst concerns are realized. Meredeth is back. I'm to go with her. Dad, as usual, seems caught between her charm and her power and says nothing.

The beautiful divorcee and her little daughter have moved back to the large suite upstairs, which is available to the two of them indefinitely.

◆　　　◆　　　◆

One weekend when I am not with Meredeth, I sit with Louise on her brick front steps, the fall sunshine in our eyes and strange new dreams on our minds. We are talking about sex as if we know something already. I am eager to tell Louise everything Meredeth has shared with me about the subject, which is plenty. Not too long ago I overheard Kirsten begging Meredeth to take over the "birds and bees" responsibility. As if she hadn't already been at it for a while, she said she would be delighted to comply. "Kirsten is still a virgin, Karin," Meredeth explained. "It's hard for her to talk about these things." Smugly I think to myself, *I probably know more about sex now than she does.*

Nevertheless, I pride myself on a certain level of morality. "There are three things I will never do," I announce to Louise, tucking my feet under me. "I will never get a divorce. I will never have a baby without a husband. And I will never have sex before I'm married."

"Me neither," Louise agrees. "It's wrong."

"How do you know? Why *wrong*, exactly?" I ask.

"Because the Bible says so."

I stare at her in surprise.

Meredeth has told me it is better not to because it complicates life. (Although so far, I note, it hasn't complicated it all that much for her. I mean, she began at thirteen! What complications has she experienced in her love life? The divorce, maybe...)

But Louise is appealing to a higher authority on the matter, and that puts an end to it.

Her mother is Episcopal and sends Louise and her brother, Dick, to church every Sunday. Does she herself go, I wonder? Her mother? But I don't ask. I have never been invited to join Louise. She doesn't seem to like it much, though she hardly ever talks about it, so what do I know?

A girl at school, not a friend, really, just an acquaintance, invited me to attend the Presbyterian Sunday school when I was younger, which was next door to our grade school. I went a couple of times and learned "The Church's One Foundation" and "Onward Christian Soldiers" while marching around the room. I didn't like it much, either, so didn't go back, though the words stuck. Words like that, with that kind of music, tend to stick, I'm thinking. Sort of like Christmas carols.

I don't know anything about the Bible, so am really awed and silent when Louise just spoke so authoritatively about what it has to say about sex. The word *wrong* seems pretty final to me but strangely baffling. There's something inside that comes into immediate agreement, like something clicking into a notch, but the "why" persists.

Louise and I decide to visit the Presbyterian church the following Sunday. There we sit and giggle at everything, particularly the fly that is trying to find a resting place on the bald head of the man in front of us. Before the service is over we are in a state of suppressed hilarity that explodes in front of the offended pastor as we lurch past him through the door.

My father is putting up with these early Sunday forays into religion; "a youthful curiosity," he calls it, and reminds me that I am a Lutheran, not a Presbyterian. When I ask him what that means he says, "You're a Norwegian, aren't you? Same thing."

The only reference I ever hear him make to Jesus is on a Saturday when he announces in sonorous tones that "Jesus is coming." He is referring to our Mexican gardener.

Dad never goes to church, Lutheran or otherwise, but when Kirsten joins a choir for the sake of the music (she, too, loves to sing) he attends an Easter chorale. He sits very stiffly with his arms crossed over his chest, head pulled back with an appraising glare on his face. He's sizing up the minister and it's pretty clear what he thinks. I am loving the music and try not to look at him.

◆   ◆   ◆

"I can't believe it! Well. So now she's seeing a much older man," Theo is remarking to herself. Kirsten has just let her in on the news. We are having lunch on a bright Saturday in the Sekuris' kitchen. The windows look out on his elaborate ornamental garden and orchard, everything today in full bloom, bathed in sparkling light.

"I met him the other day," Kirsten says. "He's at least thirty—well, maybe twenty—years older than she is. He calls himself a professional astrologer."

"A *what?*" Theo shakes her head and says loud enough so I can hear, "Kirsten, you shouldn't let Karin spend so much time with her." This is especially funny to me as I am in the same room.

As I watch her cut and rinse the huge tuna her Greek husband has just hauled out of the sea for her to can, I wonder what *astrology* is. When Sekuris M. Sekuris brings Theo tuna, her kitchen smells like the dregs of occupied Norway, and I wrinkle my nose in distaste. Kirsten sips her coffee and looks sadly out the window into the flowery backyard.

"It's ridiculous," she sighs. "Astrology is all Meredeth ever talks about anymore. She wants Penn to do my chart."

"Oh, nonsense!" Theo explodes. "That stuff is pure witchcraft. Meredeth is off the deep end. You ought to get away from her." She sniffs and sets the canning jars on the stove, stuffed to the brim with the foul-smelling fish.

◆   ◆   ◆

White-haired Penn Whitfield is a thin rail of a man with merry eyes, a mischievous, crooked smile, and a thick Maine accent. His gnarled, work-hardened hands pluck away on an old guitar while we gather around Meredeth's bedroom fireplace to listen to his whimsical stories and sing folk songs. *Sweet Betsy From Pike, Hang Your Head Over, Hear the Wind Blow,* and *There's a Joy, Joy, Down in My Heart.*

He pours out laughter as if from a bottomless well, and affection upon me as if I am his long-lost daughter. He seems intent on spoiling me. He tells me often: if I have a need and it is in his power to help me, he will. True to his word, he has several times driven like sixty to get me to my new piano lessons on the corner of Wilshire and Hoover on time. I'm always losing track of time at the Big House. He paves driveways for a living and sometimes smells like tar, but I don't care.

Gisela glowers at Meredeth's new consort every time he turns up, and with a voice strident with disapproval announces that she doesn't want this low-life setting foot in her house. Her dark eyes glitter as she shrills to Meredeth that Penn is a twice-married man with a grown son back east somewhere, and he's making Meredeth his courtesan and fool! Meredeth lifts her chin in defiance and soon Penn is living with her and Karla Ingrid in their suite upstairs. They must figure the house is big enough, big as a hotel, for heaven's sake, so why should it bother Gisela, anyway? There she and Penn drink wine, sing songs to his guitar by candlelight, and study their astrological charts with concentrated seriousness. She confesses she loves the word *courtesan,* and hopes I might aspire to it myself someday. But then, no matter what the word is, in French it sounds wonderful. I don't really know what it means in English, but I suspect it has something to do with charming men.

Meredeth and Penn are secretly married less than a year later, and I am the first to know.

It's the Saturday evening after the private wedding and we are down in her kitchen, and she is pacing like a caged lioness.

I am shocked to see the fear in Meredeth's eyes as she tries to muster the courage to tell Gisela. I've never seen her tremble at the thought of doing or saying anything, and besides, why now? Why now when they are really married and not before, when they weren't? But she is ashen-faced and wringing her hands as she paces the long kitchen before she makes her announcement to her mother. How, I wonder, could she be afraid of Gisela, who seems to have become a woman stripped of power these past few years…as hopeless, as pathetic as a bird stripped of its feathers. Though Gisela's near-black eyes smolder with rage when she sees Penn saunter through the kitchen door, he just laughs at her and lopes up the stairs to "his girls." He winks at me if I'm around to see this power-play. He isn't afraid of her, almost the same age as he is, after all, and he and Meredeth are married now anyway.

Gisela turns and strides down the corridors of her great house, muttering pitifully under her breath—no one else, it seems, listens to her any more, certainly not her husband, who has increasingly become an absentee member of the family…new woman in his life, she tells me, so he's mostly gone…but he's here now, to hear this detestable news, she had to call him away from that woman to bring him home for an emergency meeting…

But Karl seems to find Meredeth as irresistible as others do.

"Well, my darling. Well. And congratulations to you both," Karl says with what appears genuine warmth. What a handsome man he is! No wonder there are other women besides the now thoroughly addled Gisela. Clearly, there will be no emergency meeting.

Many times I have seen Meredeth wrap her arms around Karl's neck and smile up at him, crooning for some favor. I have watched with envy as he melts and gives in to her pleas. Anyone can see he is smitten with Meredeth; probably has been all her beautiful life. But he sure keeps his distance from his wife, which is easy to do in that big house. The coldness between them passing each other in those big rooms has always made me nervous, so I ask Meredeth about it.

"Oh, you know. Mother already told you, didn't she? He's in the middle of a new affair." She frowns a little and walks hastily away. *Poor Gisela Von Breuner,* I think, for she is still a handsome woman, even beneath her anxious brows.

Now, when Gisela tries to corner me, peppering me with questions about "that man, Penn," I manage to escape mid-sentence if I am clever. What can I tell her? Every time we meet in a hallway or the kitchen, she flashes that wide von Breuner smile and tells me how lovely I am growing up to be. I instantly absorb the flattery. But I can't keep up with her changeable moods or her wildly intense and esoteric conversations, though out of good manners I really do try. Something alarming is happening to Gisela, but I don't understand and don't want to know.

But whenever Meredeth is alone, on those glad occasions when Gisela is gone and Penn is out paving a driveway and about to bring in some money, I ask her every question my expanding mind can ask about love and sex. She confides again, as if retracing a long, thrilling saga, that she had her first love affair at thirteen aboard a ship while traveling to Europe with her family and has enjoyed only the most wonderful experiences with men since then. She is now twenty-five.

I can't be scandalized by anything Meredeth says or does after the shock of her divorce from Henk, so I let my imagination dwell on the mysteries she is sharing with me. No detail is out of bounds. She continues to give me books to keep me interested and informed.

It still fascinates me, though, that Meredeth and Penn had gotten past Gisela's ire and had lived together in her suite before being married. Just pushed on past. Maybe Meredith's divorce from Henk had simply added too much weight to an already disintegrating family unit. Maybe Karl's affair and Meredeth's brother's wife seeking an abortion during her third pregnancy has proven too much for Gisela's matriarchal dominance.

Meredeth gives me a different reason: *it is written in the stars.* And Gisela's star is falling.

◆   ◆   ◆

It is a cold winter afternoon. Heavy gray clouds shroud and obliterate the Beverly Hills mansions underneath, and The Big House is dripping with rain.

I am curled up on the window seat that looks out to the southwest, and I let the book *The Ideal Marriage* momentarily settle in my lap. Hot flames are licking and searing the walls of the fireplace as they emit a lusty roar up the chimney. Meredeth has just laid another log on the fire. I watch her wrap herself in a soft, brown robe the color of cocoa and braid her long, newly washed hair into a thick rope that hangs down her back. She reminds me of a dark-haired Rappunzel. Her face is radiant in the firelight, and her silky brows create even, straight lines above her wide-set eyes, those eyes that make her appear innocent and provocative at the same time.

My lashes are blond and my brows don't show at all.

A door downstairs slams shut. "That's Penn," Meredeth cries, quickly wrapping the braid in a coil and pinning it to the crown of her head. "My darling soul mate!"

Clad in peddle-pushers, saddle shoes, and checked shirt, I look at her questioningly.

"What in the world is a soul mate?" I ask, as if the words don't speak for themselves.

"God put us together lifetimes ago," she answers. "It was meant to be." Lifetimes ago. Now I remember. She has recently been convinced that reincarnation is the Great Truth of the universe, the secret nobody wants to admit answers every question ever asked. It's not that I'm skeptical; actually I'm impressed. It seems so logical, and very comforting.

She swings her legs over the bed, wraps the robe loosely around her naked body, and pads in bare feet to the door, where she meets Penn with a long, lingering embrace—too long for my comfort, and I squirm. Does he realize I am here? He looks over her head at me and chuckles. He knows I'm here, not minding, inviting me with a wink to share in their open playfulness. Meredeth turns her head and looks at me with her dark, smiling eyes. I can see flecks of gold in them from the fire on the hearth, and I smile back at them as Penn holds her against him and caresses her back with his gnarled hand. She gives a little purring growl and we all laugh.

I've been drawn in, and I love what I am seeing. I can hardly wait, I think, to be a woman, a woman in love, held, caressed, joined with my very own soul mate. Even if it takes reincarnation…

Meredeth steps out of Penn's embrace to get the bottle of wine that stands atop her library shelf. She fills three glasses to the brim. Penn takes his with a solemn bow and hands one to me. They toast me, then each other, with ceremonious smiles.

My heart is hammering strangely. I wonder how long I'll get to stay in their room with them that evening—then hope, on second thought, they send me out soon.

◆   ◆   ◆

When I was only thirteen I envied my friends who were showing the evidences of growing up. I looked for the signs to come to me with eager anticipation. But by fifteen I couldn't care less. "I told you there's no fun in it," Kirsten reminds me gloomily. "It's nothing but a curse." I used to think, how could growing into womanhood be a curse? Meredeth would never have agreed to that.

But Kirsten is right; I've watched her. Physical pain, emotional craziness. Depression; irritable, snappish conversations. I fight it, usually with success. Kirsten fights and mostly loses; she gets migraines. It seems she expresses a whole month's worth of fury at being woman, expressible only because one's period gives her a kind of universal license to do so. But I refuse to sympathize. Hasn't Meredeth taught me that it was *all* marvel? I feel confirmed in my opinion of my sister as being a progressively negative, gloomy prude, and I vow I won't, I *won't,* be like her.

I think of Mrs. Cornwell, the closest thing to a grandmother I know. Who knows how long ago she mastered this mysterious art? One thing I know: she has emerged a strong, solid, gentle woman, full of quiet strength and inner peace in the face of many personal tragedies. She lost her husband in the war. She was practically homeless in England before she came to live with us, she and her son John. She is always warm and soft, always motherly when the child inside me cries. Everything she does is with a kind of faithfulness to the task at hand, without question or inner combat, at least not that I can ever see. Her dependable industriousness in our kitchen produces love gifts like steak-and-kidney pies and rice pudding, always accompanied by the fragrance of her little sprigs of lavender.

She is in the kitchen making jam the day of the rude awakening.

It is a Friday afternoon, and we are alone in the house. I feel listless and achy, the usual, the normal. I gradually feel less and less like being up and finally flop onto my bed, pick up a *Silver Screen* to peruse, trying to ignore the tide that sucks away at my insides, dragging a burning ache down my legs. A couple of pages of Elizabeth Taylor and some blonde starlet I've never seen, and I wonder why the inner rending isn't disappearing. I can't understand why lying down doesn't make me feel better; it always has before. I throw down the magazine and close my eyes. Sleep would be good. I toss, turn, twist, knot and unknot my body. It feels like a giant roller has lowered itself onto me and I am pinned beneath the pressure. I grip the bedspread and moan, twisting my legs, raising them up and dropping them again fruitlessly. This feels like what I've heard about childbirth!

The room is getting dark; dusk is settling. The heavy, rose-clambered drapes take on an amber glow as twilight falls on them from behind. I am moaning with every breath, as if that would help, and think how moaning helps when you are nauseated and are going to throw up—then how much better you feel when you're done. I'm vaguely surprised when I see that the sheets are pulled all the way off the mattress in twists of damp, knotted bedding.

Suddenly Mrs. Cornwell appears. I am on my stomach, and I bury my face in the gnarled sheets. I feel her stout form sit down next to me, and her warm hand on my back. I sense she knows without explanation what I'm going through, and though I want to say, "Don't tell Kirsten," I'm glad not to have to talk.

"Karin, love." She's going to say something to me. I listen.

"Karin. I want you to say the Lord's prayer with me. Would you do that?"

Incredible. I can hardly breathe, much less say a prayer out loud; of all the things I feel like doing, that is the least. Besides, what if I don't know how to say it? But I can't protest. Her hand is firm on my back. The pain seems to roll in all directions until I'm pressed flat, like a woebegone gingerbread man on its face, by its weight. "*Our Father…*"

I hear her gentle English-accented recitation of the unfamiliar words commanding mine to follow. Every clause is carried by my gasp of breath; a broken-up burden of words thrust upward without feeling, only in childish obedience to the hand that presses them out of me. "*Lead us not into temptation, but deliver us from evil...*"

Her hand feels like a warm iron. Its heat penetrates into the interior folds of my body, then spreads everywhere. "*For thine is the kingdom, the power, and the glory...*"

The prayer ends. Her hand lifts, and with it, the pain. Not a trace remains in any nerve.

I am seized by an alarm of wonder. The pain is gone. I lie rigid and unbreathing for long seconds, contemplating that place which only a moment ago has been a hot torrent of pain. Now it is a smooth, cool, glassy pool of peace. "Mrs. Cornwell!"

"I know, love, I know." She pats me gently on my shoulder, smoothes down her flowered dress, and leaves the room.

At that moment—for that moment—I think there might actually be a God, one who speaks.

"*I know, love. I know.*"

I will tell Kirsten after all.

◆   ◆   ◆

Helena is our nearest neighbor, and she is a wizened gnome of a woman with crinkly eyes and a low, rumbling laugh. Her college-age son, Bill, is a friend of Meredeth's as well as Kirsten's.

Helena worked the night shift at Hughes Aircraft during and for some time after the war, wearing ear-plugs in order to sleep during the day while the kids in the neighborhood whistled and shouted. Her husband, Bill Sr., has had his career at the Auto Club all along; now he's retired and she works at a florist in town. She says she has customers in the Mafia.

They seem to me an odd couple: Bill, a tall, bland sort whose mellow temperament never alters except when he's playing poker with Dad and Sekuris; she, as colorful as a parrot. She is a good listener, always drawing out words from young people who hadn't intended to speak, like Kirsten.

Helena was raised in India, where her parents were Methodist missionaries. Her father is old now, white hair and gentle eyes shining from an extraordinarily tranquil face. There seems to be a kind of permanent radiance about him. He lives with Bill and Helena for short periods each year.

Bill will tell you Helena is a maverick, not holding to any of what her parents had lived for. She is quick to agree, though her smile about it is a little sad. She loves to tell Kirsten and me stories of her life in India, stories liberally sprinkled with the Hindu culture she grew up with. All we have to do is knock at the door and she will usher us into her comfortable living room and into a fascinating and exotic world. She'll settle us down with tea, then insert her cigarette into a long plastic holder. Her short, thin hair is dyed red or brown, depending on her mood, and her long, irregularly penciled brows are drawn a different length every day above small, piercing eyes. Her red lipstick always seems to have been applied slightly out of bounds of her thin, always smiling lips.

My father's walls come down when Helena and Bill come to visit. Her friendliness and humor relaxes him, and her interest draws him out in spite of himself. She knows how to be quiet, to wait him out while her cigarette smolders slowly in its holder.

It has been years now that Helena and Bill, Theo and Sekuris, Kirsten and Dad have had a congenial Saturday night routine of poker playing at our house. The sound of Helena's low chuckle, interspersed with Sekuris' Greek-accented lion roar, then Theo's and Kirsten's occasional cries of dismay over a losing hand, are like familiar music. They all stay well heeled in bourbon and Scotch as they play, but it never seems to do them any harm.

One night Bill and Sekuris announce they are going to do the cooking the next day. Sekuris and Dad agree to prepare a real Hungarian goulash and Bill is going to bake an apple pie. The next day the three of them congregate in our kitchen with grocery bags full of Crisco, flour, beef, paprika, onions, and apples. Kirsten, Mrs. Cornwell, Helena, and I are barred from the room. Several hours later the spicy smells begin drifting through the house and we tiptoe up to the swinging door, opening it a crack to get a glimpse of the gourmands at work.

Kirsten begins a strangled laugh but Helena covers her mouth with her hand. I want to know what's happening, since I'm standing behind all three women and can't see a thing. Helena opens the door wider. We all stare in fascinated silence. Half-empty drink glasses sit all over the kitchen. Bill and Sekuris are kneeling on the linoleum, trying to pry a ragged, flattened round of pie-dough up from the gray linoleum in one piece. Standing against the stove at an angle, as though on a ship's deck tilted by waves, Dad is swaying gently, stirring a pot that bubbles and hisses and spits over a high flame.

We etch the picture permanently in our minds, then erupt in laughter: Mrs. Cornwell's low and melodious, Kirsten's a high whine of disbelief, Helena's a gentle continuous giggle. Bill and Sekuris, still kneeling, turn bleary eyes on us. Dad smiles slightly as he stares into the pot and keeps stirring. Had he moved a hair, he would have fallen over.

The goulash burns, the pie never reaches the oven, and the men's eyes gleam contentedly as they are ushered out of the kitchen. Kirsten and Helena wash the floor and send Bill and Sekuris home.

Several times a year Helena prepares a true Indian curry, to which we are all invited. I love it immediately: the rich curried sauce over chicken and rice, the condiments of peanuts, raisins, coconut, and Major Grey's chutney. Tonight Theo and Sekuris are with us there with Dad and Kirsten. Sophia and I will go back to our house after dinner to play Parcheesi. Helena suggests the grown-ups all stay for some different kind of fun. Her eyes are twinkling.

About two hours later we hear the front door slam and my father's firm foot-falls stomp into his room. Sophia and I look at each other. I go into the kitchen for some milk and find him pouring himself a drink, his face the color of wallpaper paste. "They'll never get me back for anything like that," he mutters to no one, not knowing I am there, and swallows a large gulp of whiskey. I look at him questioningly, but he doesn't see me and disappears into his room. Sophia and I decide to wait for Kirsten.

She comes in about half an hour later. She looks flushed and suppresses a bemused excitement.

"What happened?" I ask.

"Helena did a table-raising."

"A what?!"

She explains it. They all sat around the round table in the dining room, resting their hands lightly on the edge. With eyes closed they waited for the table to rise up off the ground.

"Did it?" I try to imagine the big, heavy table in Helena's dining room leaving the floor and hovering in the air. "Oh, yes. *Way* up."

My heart pounds. "How did it do that?"

"Some kind of invisible force. Helena calls it kinetic something."

"What is *that*?" Will I ever stop asking Kirsten questions I'd rather have Meredeth answer?

"Helena can do all kinds of things like that. She believes in spiritualism. She says she can talk to the dead and she does telepathy. Especially with Meredeth." There it was. The connection.

Sophia walks over to Helena's to go home with her parents. She has a disgusted look on her face. She, like her mother, thinks less and less kindly of Meredeth. I don't know what she's thinking about Helena.

I lean forward in my bed and ask more questions, but Kirsten says she doesn't know anything more. I can tell she isn't frightened, but sort of believes it. I know she trusts Helena, and she admitted the other day she is beginning to believe in astrology. Ever since Penn did her chart—telling her she was a Virgo and *very* detail oriented, shy and methodical, then outlining dramatic details of her past—she guesses it's too much for coincidence. I saw the change in the way she listened while Meredeth and Helena chatted knowingly about their signs. She seems to be loving the mysterious attention, and, though bemused, isn't as resistant as before.

Kirsten chuckles as she turns out the light. Her red bandana is wound in place around her head, but her blond hair is sticking out in wisps, hair so fine the pin curls are slipping. "Dad was terrified. He got out of there fast." I listen intently to see if she is awake to say more, but apparently not. The room is dark and silent.

I remember his sheet-white face and know something beyond imagination has happened over there. I can't wait to ask Helena if I could try it with her. It sounds a lot like how a ouija board works.

The next Saturday I look across the hedge to see if she is home. Helena's car is in her driveway, so I slip through and knock on her door.

7

First Loves

I look up and see my teacher usher a new boy to a seat in the back row of the class. It is almost the middle of the semester and I wonder where he has come from and why he's so late. A shock of brown hair droops over his forehead, and he's wearing a baggy blue cardigan over his gray plaid shirt. Sizing him up, I decide at once he's the one I could *never* go for. This is a relief since my teacher has already warned me about my boy craziness.

His name, Bernhardt Braandt, makes the other boys guffaw. They consider this typical Dutch-German name something to be made sport of. The All-American vs. The Foreigner thing that never seems to cool down. I know if my name were more Norwegian sounding—and there are some strange ones—I would be made fun of too.

He soon becomes known as Berni, which is still amusing to the jocks. Only the nerds and eggheads have anything to do with him. But one day I discover he is an artist as well as a scholar. From his desk behind mine he keeps a series of delicious cartoons going, very much like Walt Kelly's *Pogo,* and he shares each new addition with me as soon as it is completed, wordlessly sliding it over my shoulder. I follow each episode eagerly, not missing a word or nuance of each drawing, and laugh aloud at how clever and funny they are. The quickly sketched little figures, their lifelike motions and expressions. The witty repartee exchanged in the dialogue balloons. All this drawing doesn't slow him down in his school work; in fact he's so fast the drawings are formed in his spare time. I'm not so fast in my work, so I bring my drawings from home to show him.

"They're good," he says. "Really good!" Then he smiles at me with light-filled Dutch blue eyes. I change my mind about not liking him. He asks if he might show my drawings to his mother, who is a watercolorist. I agree, and a deep sense of excitement fills me up to my chin.

Ilse Braandt sends them back to me with a little note of compliments and suggestions. I am overwhelmed by her caring attention. "I really feel honored," I say to Berni. "She didn't have to do all that."

"Your artwork really is great, Karin, or she wouldn't have." He looks at me gravely. "Keep giving me more drawings to show her." Something about that look and those earnest words make my heart pound.

From then on Berni and I spend every lunch hour together, talking non-stop. We stay late at school after everyone else has gone home. We delay going our separate ways for as long as we dare. We excitedly disclose our peculiar interests to each other. As we compare our lives we discover similarities in our backgrounds: "At our house we listen mostly to classical music," I tell him. "My father can't stand jazz." At his home Berni studies classical violin. Sometimes our family gathers around the fire and listens to an entire violin concerto without speaking, celebrating Heifetz's or Oistrakh's genius. His family does that too. We are the only family on the block that doesn't own a television; neither does Berni's. He is a European among Americans, just as I am. I don't realize what conflict that has caused to simmer in me until I see it in him. The difference is that he seems to meet the conflict head-on, without compromising himself to gain popularity. In fact, he seems immune to the lure of popularity. Is he only a boy? He practically seems a man to me. Berni, out of a mix of scientific interest and love of nature, is also a bird watcher. As I can see this simply provides more grist for the other boys' mills, I think: only a man could pass the stigma of that. But he suffers their crude remarks and general snubbing with humor-tinged dignity.

None of my friends understand why I like him, especially Louise. She laughs at my passionate defense of his nonconformist ways. I am subtly aware that she doesn't understand him because she doesn't—and can't—really know me, and why should she? There's nothing I can do about the painful cultural gap between me and my American friends, and sometimes it surprises me with its sting. I feel guilty, I feel proud, I am defensive, vulnerable, and confused. Berni is *not* confused, and Berni is my ally.

But Mrs. Cornwell understands. She watches me kindly over her cup of afternoon tea as I tell her all about Berni. Meredeth seems to understand, too. Kirsten says nothing much. Theo laughs down at me and tells me outright I am just silly.

When our music class rehearses for an á cappella presentation of early American music, I am chosen to sing the third verse of the "Battle Hymn of the Republic" solo. When it comes to the part about *the glory in Christ's bosom*, Bernie watches me evenly. I'm flushed with embarrassment but I sing it as clearly and strongly as I can, as if he is my only audience. His eyes look straight through me and I see a cloud of tears slip over them.

But the day before school lets out for the summer two terrible things happen. Someone eager to document that Berni and I are boyfriend and girlfriend insists on taking a picture of us together. I never saw it coming, but should have; his eyes have been so warm on me. He has been *warned*. Someone has said it: keep your mind on your schoolwork. Don't just think about Karin.

He steps yards away from me, hands clasped behind his back. The finished photo shows him stiffly distant, chin high, and me head down, alienated and baffled. He, my best friend, my first love, is a wall, and I am so stunned I can't speak or move. Someone…someone, maybe his father?…has told him to *back off*. Or maybe it was he, himself.

Berni follows those orders to the letter.

In spite of new friends, who draw me into their clubs and their parties and their shopping, mimicking the Hollywood ingénues we see in movies, there flows a constant, deep river of grief over Berni's rejection of me. I am so undone at the sight of him striding down the hall that I become tongue-tied and flustered. Why won't he talk to me? What have I done? More than once I stumble and drop my books with a crash all over the polished linoleum hallway in front of our lockers while Berni pretends to ignore me. I groan when I see his cold stare as he turns on his heels away from me. I feel embarrassed and stupid. I can almost see his thoughts: I have become ridiculous in his sight, I'm too much—or not enough—of something. So he has abandoned me. I cry at night, hard and long, for months. I can't concentrate on school. I am too exhausted to think.

"You are being so silly," Theo chides over the usual tuna sandwiches. Now Kirsten agrees.

So I simply stop talking about Berni. But I think about him constantly. It is uncanny, I reflect, how like my father he is, the dry personality, strong intellect, the proud, cool bearing, quick humor. A disconcerting aura of superiority. A disdain for American materialism (he still wears that baggy blue sweater) and affectation (does it ever occur to me that Berni is *poor?*). Both are great chess players and fast with straight-faced one-liners that can make a room full of people laugh.

The message at home and from Berni is this: This culture *you* live in is not *ours;* to belong to it is to be corrupted. If you fit into it you are betraying who we are, who you are meant to be. We are disappointed in you; you are too much them; you are not enough us.

The inner turmoil will not be abated; the inner questions will not be settled. If I wash the lipstick off, will they accept me? If I separate myself from the crowd and go it alone with my books, will they let me back in?

Was I ever in, anyway? If I am a foreigner in my own family, a foreigner to Berni, where do I belong?

8

The Wilderness Crossing

Mrs. Cornwell moves out the summer of my freshman year in high school to take care of an elderly lady in Santa Monica. I don't know she is leaving until she is almost gone. The way she quietly exits my life makes me wonder if she disapproves of me in some way, too. I try not to miss her—feel I have no right to miss her—and soon succeed in putting her out of my mind. It is as though this separation, too, is inevitable. Kirsten and Helena stay in touch with Mrs. Cornwell, but somehow I am never in on her rare phone calls. She lives too far away from us to visit by bus; she doesn't have a car, and she's very busy with her caretaking.

So missing her, thinking about her, is not an option. Until we receive the news about her son, John.

After joining the Navy, John eventually marries a plump, sweet girl with warm red hair, honeymoons while on leave, sets her up comfortably in a Brentwood apartment, then disappears while on an air reconnaissance over Alaska. For many months we all maintain an unspoken, stubborn hope for him. Sometimes I am drawn to make an after-school pilgrimage to the tiny home where his bereaved young wife waits for news of him. She weeps and calls me her visiting angel. But his plane, his body, is never found.

Only months later Mrs. Cornwell is hit by a car while crossing the street and killed instantly.

On hearing the news something clamps down inside and locks tight. I am my father's daughter: he doesn't speak of my mother, and I never again speak of Mrs. Cornwell.

Knowing our house will be empty when I come home, I begin a desperate ritual. I prolong the time by walking the seven miles from school to our house in Brentwood. Sometimes I follow Berni by a couple of blocks (he must know I'm behind him; we're the only ones walking that street), carefully approaching his house after he has had time to disappear inside. My heart hammers in dread and need and hope as I cross the main boulevard and step onto his corner. There it is, a modest little yellow house, the quiet exterior yielding nothing and no one. I march on, deflated and ashamed. In less than an hour I will be home, to the silent, empty rooms where I will hide away with the gnawing emptiness in my soul. For many months I re-enact this quest for a miraculous reconnection with Berni. What would I do if he appeared? What would I say?

On a few occasions his mother steps into her front yard and greets me with her thick accent and her clear blue eyes, so like Berni's, and asks about my artwork. Once she sends me home laden with a Quaker Oats container full of warm, ripe plums from their tree. Her kindness causes a spring of joy to rise in my chest. I press on, filled, the old longing quenched for a time. Perhaps she somehow understands what I am looking for and experiencing. The sense of displacement, the homesickness. Does she ever realize it is for Berni?

My father has made it very clear that America is not *home*. Norway was, and to it we must someday return…the sooner the better. I stand on tiptoe, treading lightly the southern California earth lest I send down roots from my feet that my father would uproot with the next breath.

As I walk into the empty house, I shut the world out completely. I fear any intrusion into the private realm I am beginning to build. The unexpected sound of the doorbell, or even the phone, sends me into panic. Sometimes I stand stock still, barely breathing, until the intruder (even on the phone) gives up. Then, stealthily, I slide onto the piano bench where I imperfectly but passionately pour out my soul through Chopin…Mendelssohn…Schubert…for the next two or three hours. Then Kirsten comes home, and I am dragged away from the piano to help with dinner.

◆   ◆   ◆

Kirsten has announced that she wants to go visit our people in Norway.

That means leaving my father and me to fend for ourselves for about three months, and I don't know whether to be ecstatic or terrified. For the most part, I figure, he'll be his usual elusive self, and I'll live my normal sequestered life in my room. My room…my room without my sister, for the first time in my life. I like the sound of that. Erling won't be around much, if at all; he moved in with buddies months ago.

Kirsten says this trip is a graduation gift—whether from herself with money she's socked away or financed by Dad she doesn't say. She has gotten her B.A.

degree from UCLA with honors, then her Master's degree in geology—that was what some of our summer trips to the Sierras were all about, looking at and talking about minerals, rock formations, and canyon strata until I was bored out of my mind.

I am very cautious in approaching Kirsten's plans for visiting our mother. She is cautious in return, making it sound like it isn't a big deal. That must be because, beyond the obvious visit to Tante Dagny and Onkel Anders, about which she is expressing high excitement from both sides, letters flying back and forth full of plans, Mother's condition is still vague and her reaction to Kirsten's visit uncertain. This much she admits to me: "I don't know what she'll be like, or what she'll think of me."

Though my father still never mentions my mother to me, Kirsten continues to reminisce, especially as she is packing, that from what she remembers of her that I am the one who is "so very like her." I really can't understand what she means by this. And how can she not know that her words are planting a seed of terror that I too will someday lose my mind? It doesn't help at all to know that my mother loved music, singing, laughter, "just like you do." Kirsten's girlhood memories of her add up to an explosive equation in my mind, not the soothing consolation Kirsten must think she's offering.

When she leaves with many suitcases and warm coats (it is already September) it strikes me: my sister, the only 'mother' I have ever known, is going to see *her*, not just *our*, mother. To me, this woman has always been a relative of some distant sort to both of us. Vainly I try to grasp the emotions Kirsten might have felt and is now feeling for her.

The plane carrying her up and away is out of sight. At home my father and I awkwardly set about traversing the distance between us. He tries to be cheerful, even jocular, as he comes in the door at night. We are really together only at dinner, for which I am partly responsible. Meredeth blows in occasionally to help me prepare real food, but it is heavily herbed in a way that obviously doesn't please Dad. So most of the time the center of our meal is the faithful centerpiece of Norwegian cuisine, the boiled potato. Dad says he will be satisfied if I can manage that, and he'll fill in with a seared steak or some fish. But night after night I boil the potatoes dry, burning them until they weld with the pot while I run back and forth into my bathroom to try some new makeup or hairdo. The putrid smell of those charred chunks of starch fill the house.

"Do not *leave* the kitchen when the pot is on the boil," he finally yells. Humiliated, I obey, and we get through the next few weeks with only an occasional catastrophe. But he is as surly as if there had been nothing but calamities, and takes over most of the cooking. When I try to help he growls, "Get out of my kitchen," and pushes me away.

I receive my first invitation for a real date during these tense weeks. One of my classmates' brother, a nice, solid-citizen type who dresses neatly and has manners, asks me out to dinner and a movie. Dad frowns and paces, glaring at me as if I am the cause of more turmoil than his nerves can stand. He throws his hands in the air as if an evil genie has been let out of a bottle and he can't put it back in. "Of all the times for Kirsten to be gone!" he cries. "What can I do?" I think for a minute he is going to break down and cry. Then, his voice strangled and high, "All right, all right. Go."

Tom Baker arrives at the door looking polished and harmless. His brown hair is slicked back neatly with Vaseline hair tonic, and he quickly extends his hand to Dad and introduces himself. Dad glowers at the hand as if it's a bad joke. Without looking at him he says "Bring her back by eleven," and turns away. I look apologetically at Tom for my father's rude behavior, but I feel very grown up as Tom opens the car door for me, and I smile as I settle into the seat of his 1951 Chevy Impala. He is dressed in a brown suit, red tie, and shiny black shoes.

We pull into a crowded parking lot where a valet waits to take his car keys. Tom hands them over, gets out and sprints around to open my door. Then he takes my elbow and steers me up the steps into the fanciest restaurant I've seen since the Beverly Hills Hotel. I smile up at him and say "Thank you," as he takes my coat and seats me. He orders for me, puts his napkin on his lap, and for a few awkward moments we are silent. I am not sure what more is required of me at this point on my first date with someone I barely know.

Tom has already graduated and he tells me proudly he has applied for college. Stiffly, as formal as either of us know how to be, we talk about school in a stilted exchange of sentences. His studied courtesy finally makes me laugh, and I give it up and begin chattering as much nonsense as I can dig up out of myself. He relaxes and actually begins eating his food.

But I find myself comparing him with Berni, who has become tall, exceedingly handsome, and remote as ever. As I dig into my salad I muse that not only does Berni not drive, he probably doesn't even own a suit.

I know I can never feel anything for Tom. But still, it *is* a real date, and he seems to like me.

We arrive home before eleven, and I am glad to be one up on Dad's grumpy curfew orders. Tom pulls the car in front of the house by the curb, then turns off the lights. He draws me to him for a small goodnight kiss. I gladly give it, sinking gratefully into his warm, masculine arms. I am not in a hurry to pull away…Suddenly the door on my side flies open and a strong arm grabs me by the collar of my coat and yanks me out of the car. Dad's rage-filled voice shrieks, shouts curses into the silence of the night as he drags me along the grass, tearing my stockings and dislodging a shoe.

He spits at Tom, "Get out of here, you b—!" Dad shoves me through the front door, my purse falls to the porch, and I trip over the contents underfoot. The door slams shut and the house shudders. Dad directs a volley of foul names at me. They fly around the room for what seems like minutes on end, the words lodging like knives in my soul. Then he growls like an enraged bear and commands, with a passion I've never seen—as if he's never been more determined about anything in his life—"Pack your bags now! You are to leave this house and *never come back*." Stupefied I stumble through the house, half-pushed, half dragged by my father's palsied arms, his face and voice distorted with fury. He throws me to my room. I stumble against Kirsten's empty bed and fall. My crying enrages him. "Stop it!" he shouts. "Pack up! You're leaving tonight! Do you understand? Tonight!"

Through the open bedroom window I hear Tom's car slowly roll away.

In dazed disbelief I sink to the floor. Where can I to go? I don't have a suitcase.

Choking on tears I try to tell Dad I don't have a suitcase, but the words are a gurgle. "I don't have a suitcase!" I finally scream as the tears fall in long streams down my face and neck. He is pacing like a caged animal to and fro in the living room. How am I to do what he is asking? Where am I to go? From far away, through a buzzing in my head I hear him mumble something. "All right! I'll find you a suitcase. Tomorrow!" It means that if I can't pack, I can't leave, not tonight anyway.

But he is going to send me away.

Morning dawns, thin and pale. The buzzing in my head has stilled, but I can't hear anything but my pounding heart. I wait in bed for the suitcase, unmoving. It never appears. Nor does he. Still I wait.

I don't know when he returned. I don't remember when I finally, gingerly get out of bed only to get back in. It may have been hours or days. I don't see him for a full week. But when I do it is without speech from either of us.

From that time on, for the whole of Kirsten's absence and beyond, my father and I speak from a distance and only when necessary, in monosyllables and without looking at each other. We live in the same house, but I am no longer at home, and neither is he. The severing from my father feels complete. I am disconnected from my family and the confusing world around me. Something in me that has been groping for a place to belong gives up. I think of running to Meredeth, but falter. She really isn't my home, either.

One night I hear flutes, oboes, a few gentle violin sounds drifting into my dark room from the radio in the living room. I strain to hear every dip and fall of the melody, every tremulous harmony created by woodwinds and strings. It is pure beauty, I think, and something else that penetrates to the core of me: pure truth. Everything beside it is ugly and pretentious in comparison. I sit up in bed and listen, longing for it to change me somehow. To purge me and leave me empty of all the hatred and sorrow that has taken me over. To fill the emptiness. But the music winds gently down, and all is once again silent.

That night I cross a kind of border where my father is standing with his back to me, where all hopes of belonging are behind me. I leave. Not physically, of course…I never was given a suitcase. And I still have nowhere to go.

But I really do leave in a way. Though I still go to school and attend classes, I drop out. Though I still show up at girls' meetings, I'm only there in body. I don't want to connect. I don't do my homework. In a hollow voice I agree to do a project but either don't finish it or forget it altogether. My teachers and classmates berate me, and I find freedom in not caring. One teacher sits me down in her office. In the low, slanted sunbeams of late fall I watch particles of dust float in their random way through the air and wonder if there is any pattern of any kind, anywhere.

She is speaking: "Karin. You are gifted, you are more than smart, you are bright. But look at this…unfinished, mediocre work, as if you're sleeping. You think you're going to make something of yourself? You're losing it, girl, and I'm ashamed of you. Put yourself to it, Karin, or you might not even see graduation! You are…"

Disconnect. I am unmoved.

When I emerge in the hallway a stab of triumphant joy goes through me: she said all that, and it had *no power*. I'm invincible to threats, hope, desire. I am washed clean through from the idea of accountability. She didn't kill me; she couldn't even get *to* me. I feel nothing of shame or regret. I am free.

But even within the freedom there does lurk a hint of fear: I have cut my own moorings and feel myself drifting….and for a while it feels like a holiday, this turning my back on everything and everyone, a blessed relief to be free of all striving, all struggle. But later an ominous sense of disorientation takes hold of me.

Grasping for lifelines, I discover Beethoven in the recordings Kirsten has collected and find myself in maudlin sympathy with his brooding musical pathos. From her books I begin to acquaint myself with eighteenth and nineteenth century philosophers. I connect with cynicism and ambivalence. And though much of it is beyond my comprehension it makes me feel wise. I begin playing the piano again in earnest, just for me, not for anyone else. The bad habits I'd acquired playing in solitude since I was ten are entrenched, and though it is frustrating at times to be so inept, I don't care enough to undo them. That would be work, and it is too late, and anyway, for what? For whom? I play the sad, slow, plaintive parts of Chopin and Mendelssohn pretty well, and am told by someone I have an accomplished touch. The feelings that are frozen hard in me melt and flow through my fingers; echoes not of the composers' hearts, but echoes of mine. They are playing me. And so the piano and I bind together in the solitude of overriding sound. In music I feel seen and understood. In music the murky tides that are flowing at such low ebb in me rise to meet friendly, undemanding shores.

Berni would have understood. But he's gone; he turned his back on me a long time ago.

◆   ◆   ◆

This is not to say the home I live in is a tomb. Not yet.

People come and go, boys by the drove rush in to take my attention (Dad can't exactly keep them out; he's not manning the door much anymore). If he gets a glimpse of a boy with a hooked nose and black hair he's ready with an anti-Semitic barb just—only just—out of earshot. He aims the same vitriolic denunciations at Kirsten's men friends. Coming home from Norway to this dark and confused atmosphere probably makes her want to go back.

Erling was a boarder with us off and on during his early twenties, depending on the fortunes of his friends (who now, for some reason, seem always fairly welcome) and his job status.

One evening he appears with a book he wants us to see. We all stare as he flips through glossy photos. Dad hangs back, pipe in his mouth, arms across his chest.

"Get a load of this one," he says, as of getting ready to conduct a seminar. He gathers us around the dining room table. "This," he says, pointing to hugely enlarged photos of something that looks like it's out of a Halloween movie, "proves there is life after death. *Look* at these pictures! Those are not just ghosts!" My father at some time claimed to be agnostic, but once grudgingly allowed there "might be something more". The table-lifting incident has never quite left him; I could tell by the way he shook his head and refused to discuss it when Kirsten brought it up one night.

"I want no part of any of that," he said pointing to Erling's book, "ever again."

He leaves the room while Kirsten and I stare at each of the successively gruesome, fascinating pages. The photos show filmy, body-shaped forms hanging in the air surrounding people who, by their closed eyes and blank expressions, appear to be in some kind of trance. They look deeply prayerful. One of them, Erling explains, is a medium; the others are relations or loved ones of the gauzy substance that had been called to meet with them. I study the pictures with a mixture of intellectual interest and emotional revulsion. There is nothing beautiful about these shards of insubstantial beings hanging in the air. But then I presume that photos of the living dead would be, by their very nature, incomplete and weird looking.

"I suppose it's difficult for those who have left this world to take on substance for the sake of those who need them," Erling said, professorially. "What you see here is ectoplasm, the closest thing to visible flesh the spirits can produce." He speaks so knowingly, so earnestly, making it all sound scientifically plausible. And why shouldn't I accept it? My imagination is free, no one can call me into account for my thought travels, and anyway, no one is trying to. Something in me has always believed there is more than the human senses can perceive. Something deep inside me knows that this life isn't all there is. Now I want to explore, take every path open to me as far as it will go. My mentor, Meredeth, is immediately available.

From her I learn that there's a name to our exploration: we are investigating the realm of metaphysics, a term I've run into occasionally while reading various philosophers. I note with smug satisfaction that metaphysics is a larger world by far than anything this material world has to offer. My feet are eager to leave the ground. Meredeth and Penn are determined to help me fly.

The summer weeks and school time weekends are crammed with long questions from me and complicated answers from them. And so many books! Books written by the convinced about out of body experiences, time travel, glimpses into past lives, all documented and certifiably true. To say nothing about UFO's and space kidnapping! But the most irresistible pastime is to examine the astrological reading from charts Penn has begun to map out for me: date and place of birth, longitude, latitude, Aries in conjunction with Saturn; all seductively and fascinatingly Greek to me. The map resembles an ancient navigational document, full of strange symbols and mathematical equations. It promises to explain everything about me, but of course Penn is its interpreter.

My hunger for the secrets of my past, future, character, and love life is ravenous. Each morsel of information leaves me parched for more. I grow impatient when Penn spends too long on Meredeth's chart, or on the effect of combining his chart with hers. The summer evenings are long; they take breaks and fix coffee or pour more wine. I get miserably restless; I don't drink coffee or wine. He tries to mollify me, explaining that every detail is crucial to strategizing their future and it all takes time and diligent study. "I'll get back to you, don't worry," he says.

Finally Penn agrees to set aside one whole evening just for me. It seems to take forever to configure all the signs and planets that belonged to my time and place of birth and I squirm in anticipation. I study the top of his balding head, bent low over the chart spread on his lap, and realize that Kirsten's work at Rand Corp as a cartographer—a mapmaker—must resemble that chart. At last, though I had to mentally wade through all the terminology, it seems he has told everything there is to tell about me, all that has ever happened in my sixteen years. There is a sweet, sorrowful comfort attending his revelations, and I wrap myself in it like a warm blanket. My father and sister might not understand my inner turmoil and the sad meanderings of my life but the stars do.

But quickly my thirst for more takes over and I lean into him impatiently, begging. What about that true love you see coming in the spring? Tell me again about my childhood, the loss of my mother, the war, the move to the U.S., the strained relationship with my father and sister. *Tell me again, tell me more,* I beg silently. I feel dizzy with the knowledge that a script has been written in the stars for me for which I could not possibly be responsible. Sometimes, to my annoyance, Penn laughs at me. My rapt attention is harassing but also entertaining to him in a way.

"You do have choices as to what to do about all this," he admonishes me, as Meredeth lights another cigarette. "Accept it, make the best of it, or ignore and fight it to your detriment." I don't understand a word of that. What can you do about what is already there but just—let it be?

"Still," I argue, "what I want to know about are all those predictions of the future? It really is there, isn't it?" I'd listened carefully as he had discussed the promising future in Meredeth's chart, and how it was impacted by Gisela's chart. There was such glittering hope ahead, changes in fortune, opening of doors to some nameless splendor of freedom and prosperity. Especially prosperity!

"You're right." He grins at me. "But that will have to wait until next time. From what I've seen so far," he says with a wink at Meredeth, "you're going to have quite a love life." I nearly go out of my skin with frustrated anticipation. Is there really going to be a magical love affair for me? Is my soul mate already in the wings? I plead, "Oh, Penn, just give me a little more reading, just a few minutes!"

He and Meredeth laugh as she grinds out her cigarette. "Just wait, wait, *wait*, Karin, my adorable child." Is there an edge to her voice? Is she annoyed with me? She put in, more gently, "Penn's so tired now, but we promise...really we do...next time." They are ready for sleep and want me to scoot out of their room. They wrench me free as I cling to Penn.

I leave their 'penthouse' sullenly, full of burning longings and wild hopes. Is my soul mate someone I already know? Is it Jenz, Berni's older brother, who has just this month come into my life?

At the beginning of summer I had decided, out of a mix of boredom and a desire for more music, to walk past my old elementary school and check out the Presbyterian Church's choir. The young choir director had welcomed me immediately, saying I had a lovely alto voice. During the first couple of rehearsals, I sat in the front row of fold-down chairs in the small room outside the Pastor's office, so I didn't see anyone behind me. And living pretty much in my own bubble I don't turn around to look, either. It isn't until the first Sunday morning I'd earned the right to sing in the service that I noticed how it was all arranged: the sopranos and altos on one side of the chancel, the tenors, baritones and bases on the other, men and women facing each other.

I look up. My heart catches in my throat. I think I'm seeing Berni. But no, it isn't Bernie—it's his older brother, Jenz. Berni had, a long, long time ago, told me about Jenz. Oh, Lord. A beautiful, tanned, soft-eyed version of Berni. And he is looking straight at me. Eyes meeting eyes, holding. Brazenly I hold his gaze until his eyes drop. We both blush. Then we sing.

Shyly, so very shyly, Jenz works his way around the fold-up chairs after the third rehearsal and asks if he could walk me home.

"Yes, I'd like that," I smile at him. Two or three miles of walking in the sunset would be nothing to either of the Braandt boys, I'm thinking.

Over the next months Penn studies my chart and gives me delicious glimpses, half-answers, probabilities, possibilities mixed with maddening qualifiers that both feed my hopes and torment me with new questions. It is quite possible that Jenz is The One, he asserts. The configurations point to certain planets being in the ascendancy at that moment, which suggests a romance of some strength about to develop. What is Jenz's birth date? I don't know yet, and want to kick myself. I'd forgotten to ask on our first walk home after choir practice.

"Well," Penn says, "we need to know when and where he was born before I can say any more. It looks like you have found a kindred spirit, but I can't tell how long it will last." I know Meredeth is sensing my frustration. She pulls an armload of books off her shelf and says brightly, "There's more than one way to get some foreknowledge, here!" I realize we are on a long, winding road and I'd better be patient. So much to learn.

We begin one afternoon with an exercise in automatic writing or *channeling*. Meredeth sits me down with paper and pen and says, "Be quiet for a bit with your eyes closed. Ask your spirit guide whatever you want to know. Then just start writing." I am still trying to get used to the luxury of having a spirit guide, but the thought of this intimate entity is at once intriguing and intimidating.

Can I really learn to follow this unseen being? It feels a little like being told to learn to swim…Meredeth, watching my discomfort, brightens. She must know, from long experience, how her brightening works on me.

"Better yet, let's do this. My great aunt died this year, and I've had a feeling she wants to tell me something important about her estate. Let's ask her to come through you. That way I can help you get started without your being scared about anything to do with you."

"Do you still want me to do the writing?" I ask timidly.

"Mmhmm. I'll just close my eyes and see if Aunt Gerta is nearby."

In only a few minutes my pen begins to move on its own power. It feels just like the times I've used the ouija board. But my eyes are closed, so I can't see what I'm writing. It feels like a broad, illegible scrawl. When it finally stops and I look up through slightly blurry eyes, Meredeth is wide-eyed with excitement. She's scrutinizing the paper as she paces the room.

"This is amazing! Look, Penn. This is written as only Gerta would have said it." She beams at me. "Karin, I knew you'd be a natural."

"Hand it to me—please," I say. The *please* is an afterthought; I am impatient. I try to read the indistinct message my hand has produced while my mind felt disengaged, but can only make out a few key words. "Money—soon—left to one who—" The rest is illegible to me, but apparently not to Meredeth. She grins at Penn. He laughs and congratulates me. What mysterious ceremony there is in all this hiddenness.

I feel a rush of success at my first venture. The thought of being a natural at this is intoxicating; the sky's the limit. No wonder I feel different, separate. There is a whole world—a cosmos!—accessible to me that others don't even dare to dream of. I think briefly of Theo and what must be such humdrum exist-ence…where is there room for romance of the heart or spirit? And of her sensuous, exuberant Greek husband who keeps her in the kitchen slicing up his albacore…what a strange pair. Even his song and laughter makes her scowl. What would she say if she could see me now, exploring worlds away and beyond this one? Then Helena comes to my mind. Her life is lived more out of this world than in it, I muse, as she concentrates on communicating with the nearby dead or the far-away living. She prides herself on her telepathic powers. Her irritation comes with the mundane world of her husband, Bill, with whom she admits she is bored and angry. They lead separate lives, except for the occasional camaraderie at my father's Saturday night poker games. They even sleep in separate bedrooms. ("He snores," she explained to me once.) She wouldn't be frightened of what Meredeth is saying to me.

But I feel a little afraid. The thought of being prepared for astral projection gives me a chill, as if it might require skill and discipline I know I don't have, and I hope I can put that off for a while. It would be so like me to get lost in some galaxy and not know how to get back. Anyway, what I am looking for is down here, not out there somewhere.

"There's nothing to be afraid of, Karin. It's marvelous!" Meredeth exclaims, that determined enthusiasm making its mark. I must be a coward. "You just leave your body for a while and travel the universe." She draws deeply on her cigarette, eyebrows raised in amusement. She looks at my gaping mouth and laughs. "You can come back to your body any time you want," she assures me. "In the meantime, you need to get acquainted with your spirit guide."

Once again my fears are allayed by the thought that I have my very own spirit guide. Sort of like a guardian angel, I guess, but active. It seems to me angels are passive, just watching, but doing and saying nothing. Spirit guides are obviously wanting me to let them take control, urging me upward, outward, into adventure. Maybe, while searching for my soul mate, they would help me find freedom from the burning hunger I feel inside.

Even so, as much as I try to promote this acquaintance, my guide's whispers always seem too obscure to decode. Meredeth loads me down with books that would help me open up to "the other side." I devour them. I want the same kind of spiritual experiences as Edgar Cayce. I chew on the assertions of the famous theosophist, Annie Besant. It becomes clear that not only is this material life not all there is, but this life isn't—wasn't—the only one. There have been others and there will be more.

The idea of reincarnation gives me solace…and curiosity. Meredeth, with the help of the books, explains the concept of *karma*, how everything is the result of deeds and events from the unknown past. "It's important to get in touch with that past so we can better understand the situations we're in now," she explains. Nothing happens by mistake, everything has hidden meaning. We could be released from a sense of false responsibility and guilt by knowing the past lives that had brought us here, to the families and relationships we are caught in now. All passion is from a past lifetime. All conflict and dissension is from a long forgotten distant time frame, fraught with drama and meaning.

"Even the astrological chart affirms the karmic relationship between your big sister and you," Penn said. "And even quite a bit here that clearly refers to your mother." I feel like I am looking into a magic keyhole; understanding beckons on the other side. Peace about who I am and why I am on this earth is within reach. But there are so many avenues being offered to get through the keyhole. Could a séance solve the endless riddles? I never knew my grandparents and feel awkward—even rude—calling on them. In some of the séances I sit through with Meredeth and Penn I notice that the spirits don't stay long or say quite enough to satisfy the pressing questions being posed. Meredeth always takes this with equanimity. It never bothers her if old Great Aunt Margot or cousin Lucas is tired or not willing to attend. "Some of them are earthbound spirits," she says. "They are tired a lot."

Meredeth seems to have no lack of other resources to explore the past or wrest a look into the future. I, on the other hand, find every glimpse like a single, scant, stingy drop of water on an increasingly burning tongue. Every laconic "answer" creates more furiously urgent questions. I begin to dog Meredeth and Penn for more, like a hungry child tugging at her mother's skirt for food after weeks of crumbs.

On the surface, all the prosaic normalcies of a high school girl growing toward graduation continue. No one at home has the slightest suspicion of the inner journey I am on. We are disconnected. The Thursday night choir practice, the walks home with Jenz, the in and out of girlfriends, the superficial appearance of homework and grumbled references to upcoming tests, all create a picture of conformity. But my grades slip below mediocrity, and I continue not to care. The sight of a C or even a D moves me not at all. I am gladly, willingly, without motivation. My father never looks at my report card anyway, and Kirsten simply frowns and signs it.

I think a lot about Jenz, Berni's brother, whose blushing, soft-eyed focus is openly on me. Our walks home from choir practice have become a regular thing, and we begin to hold hands, electricity running through us as our fingers entwine.

Lately we have begun to walk farther, stopping respectfully at my house to announce to whoever might hear that I am home. Then we continue up the street, past Jane Powell's house, around the corner onto Sunset Boulevard, down Rockingham Drive, which is growing dark and romantic with its tall, gracious trees and deep gardens. We give each other our first kisses there, dizzy and nearly faint with the thrill of it, hearts swelling and blooming in bliss. Jenz Braandt, older brother of the boy I've adored and lost, loves me. He writes passionate poetry to me, sends letters filled with the ecstasy of blue skies and wild birdsong and sweet life. A kind of fulfillment, like a conquest, fills my soul. We talk about music and beauty and sweet things. It never enters my mind to share my mystical explorations with him—that is a separate world of mine, out of bounds to anyone—and I sense he would be suspicious of Meredeth.

We had met at church, so sometimes we exchange subdued, respectful references to Christ. From my point of view—though I never say it—Christ is the unapproachable overseer of an unseen universe, not Christ the Savior Jenz sometimes speaks of. Meredeth and Penn, and even the writers of the books they gave to me, speak freely of "the Christ." The Christ within, the Christ we are to become, through the evolution of our souls. I feel at home with the transcendent, unapproachable beauty of that. There are no borders to that heavenly country, only mysterious, beckoning, labyrinthine roads running through it that will ultimately reach an ever-higher consciousness of love. It is a cosmic state that brooks no judgments, no frowning scruples or rules, no requirements at all. Only pure, delicious understanding and acceptance as we grow ever upward.

Jenz, however, does have scruples, a strong sense of right and wrong, and of temptation. These show up when the ardor of our kisses begin to melt us into each other, until control is almost lost, like the time we walked all the way to the beach in the dark and found ourselves alone down on the sand. He pulled away abruptly, tears in his eyes. "Rockingham Drive has cast a spell on us; we need to get on home," he murmured huskily.

I am grateful for the boundaries he sets, and respect him for it, because I have none of my own. My mind and heart are like eddies in a sea without a shore. They move with every current that flows beneath, and I want to float in the warmth of them with Jenz forever.

I finally tell Meredeth and Penn about my new love on an evening early in May of the following year. Up until then it has been my secret garden, closed even to them. Perhaps especially to them. I catch the look they give each other, as if exchanging a private message, and a warning.

They light the fire in the corner fireplace and offer me a throw to wrap myself in on the window seat. The conversation soon moves to the astrological chart Penn had been working on for me since last summer. It is a present, he announces, to celebrate my seventeenth birthday. I snuggle into my blanket, the stars and lights of Los Angeles sparkling behind the cold windowpane at my back, the fire aglow before us, shining on all our faces.

Soberly Penn unrolls the chart, its familiar contents appearing like a ship captain's navigational map, still inscrutable to me. He proceeds with the usual astrological language, none of which makes any sense to my ear, and which always makes me squirm with impatience.

Oh, please, I think, get to the part about when love will come to stay.

He gives the question guarded answers, qualifying every urgent query with an explanation about the conjunction of Mars to Jupiter and the ascendance of Aries into Taurus. Or something like that. Meredeth sits on the love seat, legs folded under her, quietly smoking a cigarette.

"I gave you Jenz's birth date," I remind Penn. "How does he figure in?"

"You are going to be in a position to marry young," Penn begins slowly, "but not Jenz. He really lit a match in you, though, both of your signs coming together in Venus." Inwardly I rage as he continues. "But it will burn out as quickly as it began. Up ahead there's someone new coming, it appears, from far away—" He frowns, studying the configurations, checking his reference book with its tiny printed tables. "Now, *that* will be a major, life-changing relationship." He gives me his crooked grin over his glasses and chuckles. "That one will really bring you into the place of personal fulfillment and change." I let out the breath I'd been holding.

"How soon?"

"By summer of next year."

I groan. So far ahead! I will be out of high school by then. Maybe even moved into an apartment with some of my girlfriends. We've all been talking about how great it would be to get jobs and move away from home.

The fire on the grate is burning low. Meredeth yawns.

"There's a warning sign here though," Penn continues. "If you marry in the next two years it won't last more than that. The stars are very unfavorable for a marriage before you're twenty-two. You'll have an opportunity when you're about nineteen, but the way the alignment of Venus to Mars sits it would be short lived, a real disaster."

How far away that seems, how remote. His warning falls on deaf ears. There are always warnings in astrology. Keeping track of times and dates when this or that will happen as a blessing or a curse makes me crazy.

Penn frowns thoughtfully as prediction after dire prediction overrides all the promises of wealth, love, travel, and fame in my creative talents that have sucked me into their hopes. He is quite sure this warning about a disastrous early marriage should be taken seriously. But I push it away. This great gift, this reading I've been waiting months for, has left a pit in my stomach. I don't want to believe any of the bad stuff, only the promise of some wonder, some glory ahead. And the idea of a predestined early marriage appeals to me, no matter what Penn says. I would make it work.

◆　　　◆　　　◆

On an autumn Saturday morning I take the packet of Jenz's love letters from the drawer in my desk and slip into the back yard before anyone is awake. The swing my father made is still there, hanging in the shade of the trumpet vine, which by now is so lush and thick it threatens to take over the clothesline. The sun is just beginning to slant its October rays through the lattice, and as I settle onto the old swing I can see dew sparkling on the lawn.

It has been a glorious summer, a dreamy season full of tender looks and loving words. Jenz and I have walked, hand in hand, for miles, exploring every curving street of Brentwood as far west as Santa Monica's Pacific Ocean Park and as far east as U.C.L.A. When the early fall rains come we run into it, almost dancing, laughing at each other's sopping heads and stringy hair. One Saturday we travel by bus to San Marino's famous Huntington Library and stroll through the rose garden, enchanted by the beauty that spreads for acres beyond the library.

One early evening he arrives at my door for our usual walk and grabs my hand extra hard. Urgently he whispers, "Come on, Karin, there's something I want to say to you, right now." I laugh and wonder why he is suddenly so serious.

"Look," he begins, "You know how much I love you. I think we should—um—talk about being married." I gasp, but he lunges ahead. "No, I don't mean right now, I mean someday. Someday we will be married, won't we?"

A curious coolness fills my chest. I pull away a little, and quicken my step.

"Oh, someday, Jenz. Maybe someday." I laugh again and put my arm around his back. "Come on, look! There are buzzards in that eucalyptus tree up ahead. Let's run and see if we can scare them away."

I don't want the dream—the dreaminess itself—to end. I can tell Jenz is embarrassed at his impulsive words, so I tease and play with him until he is smiling again.

Everyone in my family seems to approve of Jenz. Yesterday, when he walked me to the door, he saw my father hovering nearby. He extended his hand. Dad looked him square in the eye and shook it with a grip that was mutually firm.

"You look happy these days," Kirsten says with a smile when I come in. "I can see why, too." She is propped up in bed, reading her dictionary.

"He's so nice, Kirsten. He's so sweet!" I feel myself blush at the thought that it is I, not Kirsten, who has a boyfriend. She isn't partying much now that Penn is the only man in Meredeth's life, and the men who come to see Kirsten at home are rapidly dismissed by my father as being unacceptable in one way or another. I watch Dad dejectedly as he freezes one after another of them out. He is cold to the point of rudeness to them, then sarcastic to her when they limp away, defeated. It looks to me like he is more and more determined to keep Kirsten for himself, no matter how it binds her down. I know he and I have lost each other forever, and sense that his need for Kirsten has become even more intense in the aftermath of that night when he roared at me to leave and never come back.

In a real way I never have come back—because I simply can't.

I often hear Kirsten sobbing in our unlit bathroom late at night, strangled sobs that die away to low moans. I picture her kneeling against the toilet, arms hugging her head, face pressed hard against the seat in an effort to muffle her cries. I squeeze my eyes shut tight, clench my teeth, and pull the pillow over my head so I can't hear. It's probably just another migraine.

But today, while fixing breakfast in the sunny kitchen, her face is a mask of poise, and there are no traces of suffering in her eyes.

"Where have you been, pumpkin?" she asks. An endearment. So softly said, so seldom heard.

Does she love me? Why should she when I have been lain on her back to be carried all her life? What are the accolades she receives from her friends for being so strong and gracious under the load compared to the loves she has lost on account of me? Sometimes I want to spit us out of each other's lives: the burden and the guilt; the crown of heavy jewels others have made her wear because of all she's sacrificed for me. The crown of thorns I brought into her life for her to wear on her brow.

"It was so beautiful early this morning that I went out to the back yard to swing," I tell her. She glances at the bundle of letters with Jenz's handwriting on them and nods in recognition.

"I've seen those come in the mail," she says, and smiles. Unexpectedly she turns from the stove and touches my face. "Romance makes you pretty, Karin," she says. "And yes, Jenz is very nice. I like him." I feel a rush of gratitude. She approves.

"Do you think—" I venture uncertainly, "Do you think Dad would let him come to dinner sometime?"

"Well, I'll tell you what," she says, flipping two pancakes perfectly, "I'll see to it that he will." There is a grim strength around her mouth, a set in the chin. I twirl away, amazed and ecstatic.

And so, against all odds, it happens. Jenz's shyness and perfect manners must have convinced Dad that he is, for the time being at least, harmless as a dove.

Of course he has no idea, as he presides as host at the head of the table, what Jenz is like on Rockingham Drive in the dark. I smile to myself and pass the roast beef. That will always be our secret. In the meantime, on this chill autumn night warmed by the candlelight on the table, we are both our most grown-up, courteous, dignified selves. I can see Dad visibly relax, although he avoids, as always, looking me in the eye. As the peas came around the second time I feel confident that Jenz would never do anything—at least not in front of my father—to get me thrown out of the house.

And after that perfectly convivial dinner, I think maybe I will marry Jenz someday after all.

◆   ◆   ◆

My eyes widen when Jenz hands me a note from his mother, beautifully painted in watercolor. It is a handwritten invitation to Thanksgiving dinner at their house. Jenz grins at me with pleasure as I read it. "Really, Jenz? You really want me to come to your house? I mean, I already know your mother, sort of. She gave me a box of plums once when I was walking home from school." I felt my stomach twist a little at the memory of those lonely, miserable expeditions past Berni's house when I was only fourteen. "But your father, the Dutch sea captain you've told me so much about. I'm a little afraid of him, I think. You know I'm not much of a student, and isn't he going to be a professor or something?"

"A meteorologist, actually. That's why we're living here, so he could get his Master's degree at U.C.L.A. But don't worry. He's stern but kind. And he loves your drawings."

On Thanksgiving day, I spend two hours picking through my limited wardrobe, finding and then rejecting innumerable cast-offs from Meredeth, which end in a heap on the floor. I settle on a plaid skirt and deep blue cashmere sweater set that Louise bought me for Christmas last year. I desperately need a coat, and find the only one that matches had also belonged to Meredeth. I decide to wear it anyway, just for warmth while walking to and from Jenz's house. He, at almost eighteen, is still not allowed to drive and will pick me up on foot, as usual.

I put the selected clothes on hangers and bring them to our small laundry room. I will iron them later. But first, while the sun is still high, I will wash my hair. I find a lemon, cut it open and squeeze it over a small sieve to use in my rinse. As I tilt my head under the faucet, a mix of excitement and apprehension makes my heart pound. I am actually going to go in to the little yellow house I passed a hundred times in my quest for Berni. Will Berni be there? Of course he will, it is Thanksgiving.

I brush my hair dry in the sun. It is so fine it floats with electricity. I sit in a lawn chair with my head thrown forward, my eyes unable to see through the white-blond curtain before my eyes.

9

Soul Ties

Jenz is holding my hand tightly as we enter his house. His fingers are trembling. Ilse Braandt greets us at the door with a hearty, "Welcome, Karin!"

I notice immediately that she hasn't changed a bit in the years since I've seen her last. She is still short and round, with graying hair swept carelessly away from her face in a little bun pinned down on top of her head. The same twinkling eyes, the same ageless appearance unobscured by makeup of any kind, her face etched with laugh lines. No wonder I've always loved her, I think. She's the most transparent woman I've ever met.

Jenz carefully removes my coat and hangs it on a peg near the door. He takes my hand again, and I notice how moist it is.

Where is Berni? I wonder. My heart begins to hammer and I will it to stop. This is no time to even think—but—the irony, the amazement of it!—here I am again, sideways in his life, his older brother's first love. I feel somehow dishonest.

Mrs. Braandt, her face rosy from the heat in the kitchen, invites me to be comfortable for a few minutes until dinner is served. Mozart is playing cheerily on the radio. "Is there anything I can help you with?" I ask. She waves her hand in dismissal. "Ach, no, it's nearly ready."

"But you haven't met my father yet," Jenz says. He steers me into his father's study, where he introduces me to the tall, bearded man behind the desk who studies me with steady, clear eyes. In a Dutch accent he welcomes me as a sea captain might welcome a visitor aboard his ship, and I stand at attention. He smiles slightly and says, "I understand you are interested in art."

"Yes," I answer. I'm certain brevity is appropriate with him.

"I have seen some of your drawings. They are very good."

"Thank you," I say.

He gives a nod, then looks at me steadily, his bearded chin raised as though in challenge.

"Study hard." His eyes penetrate mine as I promise I will—and as though he already knows I never have. But his look makes me almost believe my words—makes me want to believe them. The interview is over and I leave the room. I feel I have passed some kind of test. Barely. Jenz is called into the kitchen for something, and I am left to sit quietly on a small couch as a Mozart minuet dances on.

Berni enters the room.

The shock of brown hair across his forehead. The sky blue eyes. The gentle upturned smile. The questioning, quizzical expression.

It is the first time in years Berni has looked directly into my eyes, without wavering, without quickly looking away and disappearing.

He assumes European formality, his eyes shadowed, nods to me with a husky "hello", and sits down in the one easy chair across from me. His violin stands propped next to him against the wall. I wonder if he practices there. My mind feels like a centrifuge. He has always been exceptional on the violin…Our eyes meet again. And hold. His eyes are taking my breath away. The sea blue of them. Like Jenz's, only more piercing. The original eyes. He is halfway trying some conversation, but there's a buzzing in my head and I don't want to try my voice because I know it will shake, like my breath. A hurricane is roaring through me.

A spider crawls across the arm of the chair and stops near my hand. "Look," I blunder, as if I've found something marvelous to share with him, something we would have in common during this inconceivable moment. A spider at its center, like conversations we used to have. But Berni keeps looking at me, and I can't read his face. His image is so distinct to my heart, so intrusive, it pulses and is blurred. Timeless minutes pass. We enter into a patchy dialogue about this spider, spiders in general, and I ask stupid questions. I don't care what his answers might be, only that they be spoken in *his* voice, because the old sweet love is singing deep, clear, unchanged, unchangeable. Too shocking, too amazing—and too impossible—to bear. Why was I not prepared for this?

Jenz comes to usher me to the table and sits down beside me. But it is too late. Tears gather like stinging nettles in my eyes, and I gulp them down one by one with my food. I want to tear away from the table and run out the door, but I can only chew and swallow. Quiet conversation is going on around me, about turkey and stuffing and what kinds of treats the Dutch serve on holidays, and I hear it through a haze, the same way I always heard Norwegian when spoken at our table. I don't know what anyone is saying. I can't look at Jenz, or his mother, or the sea captain. So I lower my eyes and eat. My ears hear—only Berni.

I go home dazed, like someone stumbling away from a wreck. Accusations fly around inside my head. I have deliberately beguiled Jenz from the beginning. I took him as a substitute for Berni. Selfishly I lied in order to recapture what I could of him, to fill the void once held by Berni's voice, his quick humor, his open admiration and affection. Jenz now seems like a phantom, fading like a ghost behind the re-emerging reality. Jenz—a substitute. And I have made him love me.

I can hardly bear him now.

So, abruptly, I withdraw from him.

For weeks Jenz's eyes and voice and touch pleads with me for understanding. *What has happened to you? Why are you crying? What have I done?* I can't answer, I just walk away quickly before I'm forced to betray myself. How could I ever tell him what has happened?

The last letter he writes me is a short note, which arrives in the mail a month later.

> *My Dearest Love*
> *I miss you so much.*
> *I keep wondering what I did.*
> *I keep asking God why you changed.*
> *Karin, you need to grow up.*
> *To let Jesus into your soul.*
> *I will always love you.*
>
> > *Jenz*

How dare he preach to me like a priest, telling me I need to become a *real Christian*! What does he know about the needs of my soul? What does Jesus have to do with anything? Especially this unspeakable conflict?

I sit down and pen a cold response.

> *Dear Jenz,*
> *Thank you for your note.*
> *I'm sorry about everything.*
> *But religion is a very private thing*
> *And I don't need you to tell me what I need.*

I can't sign it "Love, Karin." Just "Karin."

I am now hardened over; both to the pain I am causing and the misery I feel and can't disclose to anyone. Poor Jenz. If he thinks anything, let him think I have fled because he impulsively asked me to marry him on one of our last walks before the dinner at his house. That his proposal had frightened me away. He could blame the dissolving of our love on himself once he thought about it enough. The business about religion had to be just his wounded pride rising up.

I tore up his offensive note and threw it away after one reading. For the remaining weeks of that school year I avoid him. When we do meet, I see by his swollen eyes that he has been crying.

My graduation from University High is still a year away the day Jenz and Berni dress up in their gowns to receive their diplomas. I move through the crowd and find a seat alone on the bleachers where I can see the graduates of summer 1954 file down the long series of steps onto the platform at the edge of the ball field. There they are, the Braandt brothers, the elder leading the younger, who has skipped a full year in order to graduate with him. No surprise there; Berni is an A plus student. Their father, Captain Braandt, has received a grant to study meteorology in British Columbia, and the family is moving from southern California as soon as the graduation ceremonies end. I learn this from a mutual friend, who, when he looks in my eyes, seems to understand something. He has known me from the beginning of Berni.

Jenz is taller than his brother and walks straighter, his eyes unswervingly ahead. Berni walks pressed forward, as he always has, as if he is about to break into a run. His full mouth is set in a firm line, as though urging himself away from all this ceremonial silliness in order to thrust headlong into the new life ahead. They take their seats somberly, and I fix my gaze on each of them in turn. Jenz, the gentle, tenderhearted poet and lover whose heart is still broken; I can see it in the shadows under his eyes. Berni, the brilliant academic and musician, the comic wit and artist, who has watched Jenz suffer and probably hates me. Both from another culture, no more at home among their peers than I, but so secure in themselves, so excellent in their disciplines that they have earned high respect in spite of their non-conformity.

When each is called to the podium to receive high honors the audience gives a roar of congratulations. The tears that have been pushing up behind my eyes spill in a sudden downpour. Someone nearby looks at me, and I get up from my seat and stumble out of the stadium. I find a corner, hidden behind the girls' gym, where I fall in a heap and let the sobs shake and split me. No one sees me, and it is nearly dark when I pull myself up and begin the long walk home.

Every night of my senior year I cry myself to sleep. Every day I weep openly in the halls between classes, careless of concerned eyes, but no one says anything. If there are studies to attend to, conversations to engage in, assignments to hand in, they are attended by an automaton in place of me that speaks, and dresses, and eats, and reads, as required.

One night Erling comes home after I have gone to bed. We are alone in the house for some reason. Who knows where Kirsten or Dad are.

He comes to my bed, sits beside it, and places his hand on my head in a stern gesture of appeal. "Karin, stop it. You must never love anyone that much. *Never.*"

I sit up, so bleary eyed I can't see Erling clearly. How does he know about this? Who does he think I'm grieving?

"It's not good to love someone this way," he repeats. "It has to stop."

In a stunned moment, his message sinks in: Love makes you stupid. I remember Theo's words: "Oh, Karin, you are just being so *silly.*" It has been five years since then...and maybe she was right. The heart is so silly. Five years! I must never love that way again. I shudder, and the tears dry suddenly.

Erling talks for a while more, then gets up, shuts the bedroom door and is gone. I lie still and stare at the ceiling.

Meredeth and Penn have little to say to the torment of my seventeenth year. They'd seen it all in my horoscope, so, though it was sad, it had been inevitable, hadn't it? They remind me of this often.

They try to distract me with new adventures into the realm of the paranormal and supernatural, and I am too tired to protest. A strange mix: hope and fatalism vie within me. A banquet of -osophies and -ologies are offered to me, and I nibble half-heartedly at them all. Meredeth presents me to her friend the palm reader, who studiously pronounces that I have a very short lifeline and probably won't live far into middle age. In the lines of my clenched fist she sees three children. I swallow her words whole, feeling powerless against the forces coming at me from all sides. Penn has been learning the mathematical intricacies and portents of numerology, and Meredeth has met a woman who offers to unleash the mysteries of my confused life by means of phrenology. So one afternoon I sit obediently in a chair in Meredeth's and Penn's new, cramped quarters in an old Beverly Hills duplex, letting her friend, Cassandra, examine the bumps on my head. She probes and measures, issuing little "ahs" and "mms" as her fingertips explore the relief-map of my skull.

"Oh, you are certainly very, *very* sensitive. Musical, artistic. A real lover of high beauty, of nature. Prone to deep unhappiness," she murmurs contentedly, as if having come across a real mother-lode of information. "And—I'm sorry to have to say it, but it's all here—a tendency to carelessness."

Prone to carelessness. Meredeth and Penn are nodding. I resent Cassandra for speaking it. I get up, and the three of them invite me to join them for some lunch. Meredeth has made a salad and some boiled eggs. In spite of the negative judgments issued about my character, high-pitched camaraderie swirls around me. "Play something for Cassandra before she leaves," Meredeth implores, waving toward the old upright piano that used to be in the sunny breakfast room at the Big House. "Oh, yes, please do." Cassandra agrees. "I've heard so much about your musical genius."

Musical genius? How could that ever be possible? But flattered into being center stage, I sit down and begin a complicated Chopin *Etude,* stumble, and began again. Then it flows from that well, almost empties onto the keys.

"Oh, what a touch she has!" Cassandra remarks. "She's really brilliant, isn't she? Does she have a guide to teach her, from the other side? She must have." Before I know it, all pairs of hands are on me and I am urged to go into a trance where I can meet the teacher from the other side who will personally bring me to perfection as a concert pianist. Soon Meredeth, Penn, Cassandra are in a trance, which makes their voices sound syrupy and their pronouncements like heavenly edicts. Minutes on the old clock tick on as I sit hunched over the keyboard under a weight of anticipation.

"It's Chopin himself who is your teacher," Penn announces. "He's right here, and he wants you to be his virtuoso! He wants to tell you he'll guide your hands, play through you. All you have to do is to relax and let him have your hands and the keys."

There are awed exclamations all around, and I can't help but smile. Chopin? My very own personal piano teacher? "But you're going to have to practice being in touch with him," Meredeth warns. "You've been given a great gift. You'll need to meditate on him, really listen for him." Her hands are heavy on my shoulders, pressing down.

I take this to mean I have to work harder to enter the trance state they all know how to do so easily, like slipping through a wide-open door. Then I realize that it is *carelessness* that lies like a soggy gauze over everything in my mind and soul. I don't—can't—care enough to push it back.

And I don't have the energy to be anyone's piano student. Not even Chopin's, though he might have traversed the leagues of death to offer himself to me.

PART III

The Upset

10

Deceived

"Karin, I'm sorry. I have to give these catalog cards back to you to retype—there are just too many mistakes."

I sit at my desk next to the south window of the Catalog Department of UCLA's main library and take the stack of three-by-five cards back to redo. This is the second batch today. Mrs. Elder, the supervisor, seems embarrassed, and it is clear she's been stretching her patience to accommodate me. My sister has gotten me this job after my graduation (Dad has refused to even consider sending me to art school, though I have pleaded) and after six months I still can't seem to get through a day's work without a hundred mistakes. Either I make stupid typos, or misfile the ones I've redone, or just can't concentrate and am caught daydreaming, staring out the window. It is too easy to relive the ecstasy and the agony of the summer just passed, too hard to tear my mind away from wondering why.

I feel bad about my failure at my first job. Kirsten pulled strings to get me here, where she herself worked before going to Rand Corporation as a highly skilled map-maker during the height of the Cold War. I know I am letting her down; that I am embarrassing her.

Kirsten has been living away from home for a long time now, in a tiny apartment a couple of miles away, and I mostly see her on weekends. When she came back from Norway during my junior year she seemed satisfied, but a bit sad, and didn't talk about the trip much. Instead she quietly shared her huge portfolio of slides, showing off the spectacular scenery of Norway from south to north, as well as her startling gift for photography.

Soon after my break with Jenz she began looking for an apartment, making the most aggressive break with her old life and roles possible. Sometimes I saw her studying me with a kind of sad resignation in her eyes—as though she knew, for better or for worse, that her job with me was done, she could do no more. She spoke of Mother hardly at all. Now she seems a bit preoccupied with her health, and once I absently catch her studying a mole on her left thigh in a clinical manner. But she doesn't seem alarmed by it, so neither am I. Anyway, when she moved I was as eager to be free of her 'mothering' as she was ready to turn from us and live her own life.

Dad looked blanched when she walked away. But the countenance of resignation so familiar to us shadowed his eyes, and he built bookshelves for her. I celebrated her tiny studio abode and her new cat, a big, fuzzy black cat with round gold eyes she named Cleo, and I took full possession of our old bedroom without a backward glance.

I see Mrs. Elder walk by my desk and smile at her. She glances at the pile of cards next to my typewriter, but politely smiles back. The people here seem to like me in spite of everything, I think. They keep telling me how pretty I look and how different I am from my shy, meticulous sister. That was one of the things that had showed up on Kirsten's horoscope. How detail conscious and orderly she is. It irks me how respected she has always been for those orderly, careful, dutiful ways, how admired for her self-sacrificing role in my life. How often I've been reminded that she's had to put her life on hold on my account. How often I turned away from her in irritation, thinking how dull all that bondage to duty is. But mostly I chafe at being the reason for it. Anyway, they must have expected her clone when they hired me but that sure isn't what they got.

I turn again toward the window, letting the beauty of the university buildings and the neatly manicured lawns soften the hardness around my heart. The tall buildings cast shadows across the quadrangle, towering, aristocratic monuments to the pursuits of intellect. The sky is glowing deep pink with the late-afternoon winter sun, and clouds drift across it, translucent on their edges. Just being here makes me feel like I am an aspiring student. I will to wrap the ambiance of university life around me and wear it as though I had earned it. I know it's pretense, but…who cares?

The contemplation turns bitter as I rehearse again the events of the past months, the weeks of secret joy followed by weeks of confusion and rage.

The man Penn and Meredeth had predicted would "come into my life from far away" had indeed come. All the way from New York, right at the beginning of the summer following my graduation. They had introduced me to him themselves. I had worn my best new pale-blue dress, my highest heels, and an upswept hairdo for the blind date at Penn and Meredeth's latest rental in Benedict Canyon. Bill was tall, dark haired, and dark eyed. Something about those merry eyes and crooked grin reminded me of someone. I looked sideways at Penn, and he threw back his head and laughed.

"You see it, don't you, you sweet rascal? Karin, this is my son, William Chase Whitfield." He bowed and spread out his arm as if presenting a princess to a prince. It didn't matter to any of us that he was twenty-eight years old and I was only eighteen. After our first secret dinner together with Penn and Meredeth, a gala celebration with steak and wine and Meredeth's famous California salad, we were a pair. He danced and romanced me as Vivaldi strummed a punctuated baroque cheer from the record player. Bill talked animatedly about the cancer research he was doing at the Sloan Kettering Institute. He was sophisticated, knowledgeable, humorous—and so very attentive. For three secretive months we saw each other every day (all arrangements courtesy of Meredeth and Penn) and I was flung into a whirlwind of dinners, theatre, concerts, light years beyond the adolescent heartache so recently left behind. He picked me up for lunch at the university and squired me away after work, back to Meredeth and Penn's for evenings of wining and dining and hilarity.

Dad never questioned my whereabouts. Being with Adele and Penn more than at home had been a long-established routine. Even though I felt a bit furtive, that only added to the sense of adventure.

Bill returned to New York, the three month vacation in California over, but with solemn promises laid at my feet. On his last night we dined on lobster, danced, kissed, and were led by Meredeth and Penn in smiling tandem to a guest room prepared for our use.

We pledged ourselves to each other; he called me his soul mate.

And then he left.

But he wrote every day. A letter, sometimes two, appeared in my mailbox at work, declaring his thoughts, his desire for me. Every day for the next three months my letters match his line for line, a continuous, unbroken weaving of love-words. I was consumed by the anticipation of the letters and the joy of responding. Then, one day, nothing. And the next—and the next. Two weeks, then three.

For weeks, I rushed to the mailroom in search of a letter. Was he all right? Had something happened to him? There was no clue. I called Meredeth and Penn two, three times a day. They hadn't heard from him, either.

"You've got to go back there," I ordered Penn, finally. "Something's wrong. I'll give you my next paycheck for airfare." He accepted the money without an argument (they were now always short of cash) and he flew back to New York the last week of October. Less than a week later the phone at my desk rang. It was Penn.

"I'm back. How about I meet you at the quadrangle in front of the library after work?"

"Oh, Penn! Where is he? What has happened to him?" I was fighting hysteria.

"Calm down," he said tiredly. "I don't know much more than when I left. We'll talk later."

We perched on a brick ledge near a grassy hill, and he picked at his calloused fingertips as he spoke, not looking at me. His voice was somber. What he was saying was simply impossible.

"I found Bill at home but was not even welcomed inside."

Standing beside the open door Bill had briefly explained to Penn that he'd come home to New York to find his socialite girlfriend from the year before pregnant with his baby. She had pressured him, threatening to expose him to his "blue book" society relatives, and he had relented.

He was now married. He would not be seeing or talking to any of us again.

It is five o'clock, and I've only finished half of my stack of catalog cards.

I look out the window again, taking in the wide expanse of the western sky, luminous with the clouds that are standing between me and the setting sun. They are motionless now, as if hung there by an invisible hand for me to ponder. I gaze, searching for something.

A crystal-clear thought comes to me, and I pull a piece of paper onto my desk and take a pen.

> *There is a great order behind those clouds.*
> *And so there must be for me. I must find it.*

As I gather my purse and straighten my desk, I fold the sheet of paper and slip it into my coat pocket.

11

Dead End

"Dearly beloved, we are gathered here before God and the face of this company—"

To be seen. To be watched. A multitude beholding...me.

In a shimmering white dress edged in embroidered flowers, I see a captivated audience watching me act out the rites of the Church, lifting my radiant face to my fans. I've wanted to be seen, dressed like this, all my life. The princess revealed.

Kirsten is standing behind me in the little bridal room of the church overlooking the sea, buttoning the last of the long row of satin-covered buttons on my dress.

"Done," she says, and gives my shoulder a little pat. "Are you ready for this?" She reaches for the veil.

How strange it is to enter marriage before you, I think, looking at her blond head bent behind me in the mirror. I'm not yet twenty; you're nearly thirty-three. I feel a hot flush creep into my cheeks.

Milt had asked Dad for permission to marry me, and he had given his consent almost without a blink. Later I heard Kirsten raise her voice in a wail of opposition, which was counterattacked with a belligerent shout. "Kirsten, it's none of your business. I want her married and off my hands before—"

I hadn't heard the rest, but had fled back to my room, shutting my mind to the conflict. I remembered bitterly what Dad had said to me when I asked if he would allow Milt and I to marry.

"Allow?" he had said humorlessly. "I'll pay the guy to take you."

The night before the wedding, as the dress was undergoing its last fitting, I break down and confess to Kirsten in a whisper, "There was someone else—last year—but I lost him. I just have to get on with my life." Trite. That sounds so trite. But how else can I say that I have nowhere to go, can't go on living at home, can't support myself away. Those high-school dreams of sharing an apartment with girl-friends have vanished, just as the girls themselves.

Kirsten turns away stiffly, nodding as if she understands.

I know my relationship with Bill had stayed secret, so she's probably thinking Jenz was the lost love. But no matter, she heard Dad's determination that I was to marry immediately. "I'll pay the guy to take you" echoes in my ears. Did Kirsten hear that, too?

Organ music is penetrating the closed door of the dressing room. I check my image in the mirror, and smile up at Kirsten. For a moment our eyes lock.

"You look beautiful," she says simply.

"So do you, Kirsten." And she does.

She picks up her white gloves and clutches them for a moment. Her eyes dart around the small room, looking for something.

"What's wrong?" I ask. "Everything is here." She takes a deep breath and puts on the gloves, then reaches for her small bouquet of pink roses. She looks down at them and I see tears glisten on her lashes.

"My bridal bouquet," I prompt her. Her hands shake as she hands it to me. Mine are steady as I look once more in the mirror and brush a stray curl away from my neck.

"All set," I say.

The trumpeted prelude of the Wedding March draw us forth to the place where my father stands waiting for me, tall and erect as a statue. His eyes stare straight ahead as I slide my hand into his crooked elbow and I feel the wooden, unyielding stiffness of it. We have never linked arms before.

Kirsten almost trips as her ankle gives way, but she recovers herself and takes her place in front of me.

The music demands that we move ahead. I step forward, nudging Dad's arm with mine. We begin the long walk toward Milt together.

Meredeth and Penn catch my eye. They are not smiling.

Milt and I spend our honeymoon in the small apartment we have rented near the campus. Our first night together. As he sleeps I lie beside him and weep quietly, tears falling like rain down my face onto my pillow. Will there ever be an end to tears? Then, in my anguish, I find the words *God is love* repeating themselves over and over in my mind. Meredeth has often used these words, flinging them around lightly as if to assign benevolent approval on all things.

But there is surprising comfort in them just now, and finally I whisper them, chanting, until a blanket of peace covers me and I fall asleep.

◆　　◆　　◆

I keep my job at UCLA, not doing well anywhere, but after several moves from department to department I finally find my niche in the Office of Public Information, where I begin to wear the role I've chosen: the bride of a handsome and brilliant graduate student of chemistry. Of course Meredeth and Penn are appalled. They remind me that, according to my chart, this marriage is doomed to failure. They seem determined that I remember that. But I won't hear it.

Besides, astrology is beginning to make me feel uneasy. Some of what I have listened to as they poured over their own charts has given me chills. One night I had overheard them searching for the astrological configurations that would indicate Gisela's death; Penn was sure it was imminent. Money would come from that, and freedom from the oppression of her disapproving tongue. I'd seen a jubilant glint in Meredeth's eyes when they thought they'd found the right signs.

Meredeth and Penn stay clear of us for the most part those first months, and I settle in to the routine of work, playing house, playing bride. But one day she calls me with an urgent excitement in her voice. "A fabulous woman lives right next door to you," she says. "She's a famous clairvoyant who does life readings all over the world." Instantly I am charged with interest. A "life reading" would reveal all those past lives I somehow know I've lived, and the meaning of them as they relate to this life. Because surely, this can't be all there is.

"Of course, she charges thirty dollars an hour," Meredeth says. "But you can manage that, can't you?" That's a whopping amount of money, I think. What would Milt say? Without consulting him, I decide that, since I am working, part of that money is mine to do with as I pleased.

"Make an appointment with her right away," Meredeth urges. "She's going to Europe next week."

I call Lotte Von Strahl and schedule a one-hour life reading for the following Saturday. Milt will be working in the chemistry lab anyway, so he won't know. He doesn't say much about Meredeth's interests; being a scientist, metaphysical explorations don't lure him at all, and I think he just tolerates mine.

Von Strahl is unusually tall and seems quite old—at least in her sixties. She lives in a dark, heavily furnished apartment with her wheel-chair-ridden husband, who nods in a sightless way when she introduces us. She has a loud, strident voice, a clipped German accent, and an aristocratic manner.

"I was in Germany during the war," she explains after seating me in the cramped living room. "It became dangerous for us there, so we moved to Africa. There the police employed me to find missing persons with great success. Since then I've lived all over Europe on similar assignments."

Having thus given me her remarkable credentials, she turns her attention on me. I lean forward, giving her as full a view of my soul as I can reveal and her psychic senses can perceive.

The hour turns into an hour and a half, my thirty dollars into forty-five. Lifetime after lifetime rolls backward, each a drama of Steven Spielberg proportions, all tied darkly together with my present relationships. "Kirsten was your executioner during the French Revolution," said Von Strahl. "This lifetime is her penance, to take care of you until her death." I feel a little aghast, and strangely pleased, but frown solemnly, thinking how apparently immutable the justice of karma is.

She asks if I have any fears. "Of water? Of horses?" I nod. Horses terrify me, and I've always been afraid of water. "You drowned in a sailing accident in 1804 and you were thrown from a horse when you were one of the ladies-in-waiting in Queen Elizabeth the First's court." Then she adds, "You were a friend of the Virgin Mary. You knew Jesus but were an unbeliever." She ends with, "You were in Germany in your last life—a man. You committed suicide." I ask for a drink of water. Deep thrills move through me at the thought of my soul's profound and colorful history.

But as I drink the water a strange sentence intrudes itself in my mind, accompanied by an image of Jesus on the cross.

If reincarnation is true, how much more will I have had to die—to break the fruitless cycle of mortal rebirths.

A picture of a rat pedaling the wheel in its cage stood before me. The futility of an endless, hopeless succession of lifetimes, good karma attempting to equalize bad karma, cause and effect ceaselessly creating new births, lives, deaths, rebirths—and earthbound souls.

Jesus on the cross.

These mystifying words and images slip like a wave past my consciousness, yet leave an indelible imprint buried beneath.

I pay Lotte Von Strahl and prepare to leave. She points to her husband, who has wheeled himself back into the crowded living room. "He is my burden from my last life. Soon he will die and I will be free at last." She gives the old man a disdainful look. "I can hardly wait."

I walk into the sunshine of that warm September afternoon and breathe deeply. Everything makes sense now. All those lifetimes I'd spent doing, and paying, and learning. Of growing. I feel very wise. And *old*.

I feel sorry for my sister. *But really*, I think, *Von Strahl said she'd had me beheaded!*

◆   ◆   ◆

The famed Roger Wagner Chorale has opened a special noon-hour choir specifically for employees of the U.C.L.A. campus, and I am wild with excitement to join. Once a week I run in my spiky heels from my office in the Administration Building to the Music Building, gulping down a sandwich on the way. In the spring we will be performing the *St. Matthew Passion* by J.S. Bach.

I am newly pregnant when rehearsals begin in September, but by twelve o'clock the morning sickness, exacerbated by the smell of thirty-two cups of brewing coffee, has subsided enough that I can concentrate on the music.

The complications and disciplines of ancient five-part harmony with orchestra, the over-and-over studious polishing of phrases, all one hundred voices brought under the authority of the maestro—it is so wonderful I fly back to work on wings. I don't know who St. Matthew is, but the biblical words and mathematically precise baroque music, powerful and tender at the same time, swell within me as we sing. It resonates in my head as I work.

The night of the concert comes with a flurry of activity backstage. Royce Hall is packed, and to my incredulous eyes there, in the very middle, sit my father, Milt, and Kirsten! The overhead lights of the huge hall cast shadows under her eyes, but Kirsten looks serene. She's recovering from exploratory surgery under that mole—there was cancer—but the doctors said they removed *all* traces, including several lymph nodes. Briefly I recall the strange physical therapy machine she uses every day to prevent lymph pooling up in one leg. And she's under orders to walk seven miles a day, on top of that. "But you know how I love to walk," she had told me, her smile bright. "I'll be skiing next winter, I promise." I believe her.

I watch them as they sit in the huge audience, talking, laughing, waiting, looking at their programs. I shift a little in my place among the hundred other singers, hear the stillness fall as the lights dim and the conductor bows, and feel an overwhelming surge of warmth fill my chest. The orchestra begins. The royal majesty of Bach's *St. Matthew Passion* takes over, lifts, and carries me into itself. I nearly weep when the orchestra makes its final dive into the sorrowful, soaring strains of *"Take Now Thy Rest, O Savior Blest."*

For weeks after I am in a state of inexpressible euphoria. Milt laughs and wonders if I'll ever come down.

◆   ◆   ◆

Kirsten is being forced to take a leave of absence from her job at Rand Corporation. There are complications following her surgery in mid-April. I'm assuming, since she gives me no details, that it's just post-op, post-cancer fatigue. Because they got all the cancer, her doctor said so. Sadly, she gives up her apartment and moves into a friend's home in Beverly Hills. She will housesit for them during the year they will be in Europe, then she'll find a new job, and a new place to live. With her credentials I know that will be easy.

"At least I get to bring Cleo with me," she says, scooping up her golden-eyed black cat. "And it's just temporary, anyway."

"Milt is signed up for a night class in German at Beverly Hills High on Tuesday nights. I'll come and visit you then," I say.

"You can join me on my walks," she suggests. "I have to put in those seven miles every day or else. It was easier when I lived closer to the beach." She glances at my bulging abdomen. "It'll do you good, too."

We chat easily as we stride together down elegant, curved streets. I describe every item I have received at my baby shower, gossip about the lewd jokes and laughter included in the party, and comment on how surprised I am at the way some of these office girls talk.

"Office girls," Kirsten remarks, "can be a pain in the neck." She begins telling me about a Swedish girl at work named Kathy. "She's been driving everybody in the office crazy, including me," Kirsten says, shaking her head. "She won't leave us alone. Before I took this leave it got so I dreaded going to work."

"Why? What does she do?" I ask as we march along. It is hard keeping up with Kirsten. Even with legs swollen hard like tree trunks she sets a formidable pace.

"Every day she collars someone and asks if they're *saved*," she says.

"Ooh," I breathe. "I know someone in my office who's sort of like that. She's this really humble girl who sits across from me, too innocent and shiny to be real. She's so sweet she repels me." I pause, reflecting how detached from the rest of us this girl is. "I don't think any of the others in the office like her, either."

As we walk I remember a conversation Marcie and I recently had. At my curious request she had patiently explained what 'being saved' meant. But I didn't understand it, and what I did hear sort of turned me off.

With Mrs. Cornwell it had been so different. She'd never talked about God. Just that one time when she had asked me to pray—when I'd had those cramps. Long ago, out of childish curiosity I'd asked her who Jesus was anyway, and she'd said simply "the Son of God." That seemed remote enough, and I didn't question it. It had felt like some immutable truth, but nothing to do with me.

"Anyway, I know just what you mean about this Kathy," I say as we round another bend away from the elegant house Kirsten is staying in. It feels good to sympathize with Kirsten. We have so rarely been on the same side of an issue. Besides, her being besieged by a religious fanatic while she is so ill makes me mad.

Kirsten is studying me, her eyes concerned. "Let's turn back," she says. "Three and a half miles is more than enough for you."

"I think you're right," I say, panting.

As we step into the driveway I see that Kirsten is limping.

12

Sudden Death

It is a brilliantly hot day where we live on the East Bay of California in July of 1958. Walnut Creek is a small, flourishing bedroom community, a suburb of Oakland and Berkeley, home to commuters to jobs in San Francisco, Richmond, Concord, and other towns within a fifty-mile radius.

I say good-bye to Milt as he pulls out of the driveway on his way to work, then turn back to the little house that is our first real home. He'd picked it for us as soon as he knew he had a job in the research department of Shell Development Co. Milt's career is on its way now, his long years of post-graduate studies at UCLA behind him. While I waited at my father's house with our new baby, Milt scoured the Bay Area for a rental house we could afford, and in June we enthusiastically began setting up housekeeping. I am a bit let down by how little we have in the way of furnishings, but know that for the time being we can't do anything about it.

I scoop up three-month old Grant and hold him in my lap, settling in to give him his breakfast bottle. He is rosy and white-blond, round blue eyes the exact shape of Milt's. He smiles at me around the nipple of the bottle, making white bubbles, then blinks sleepily and gets on with the business of sucking hungrily. Soon his eyes are closed and his long lashes lie in a fine, shadowed fringe on his cheeks. I can't get enough of staring at him, marveling at his pure, innocent beauty. It occurs to me that I have never been around babies, never actually held one until my own. I had only stared at Meredeth's, of course, a long time ago, and only for a little while. I had almost not dared to touch her, she was so like a fragile doll.

The first burp is ready to come up, and I lift him over my shoulder, pressing his warm body close to my neck, and pat him gently. I can see across the street from my front window. Young trees, newly planted, line the house-fronts like slender sentinels dressed in summer greenery. The small tract was built along straight streets, with look-alike front lawns behind those look-alike trees. My eyes scan the skyline. There are no old acacias spreading their limbs over any rooftops.

I change Grant's diapers and lie him down in his crib. It is second-hand and plain. The room is sparsely furnished and still dark in the curtained, early-morning light. There are no pictures on the walls, no cheery decorations of any kind. I close the door.

Alone, I listlessly fix toast for my own breakfast and settle back on the couch to eat it.

The young trees, their summer leaves shimmering, sway with the hot breeze beyond my kitchen window. For a moment I watch them absently. Then, numbly, I begin the morning routine: pick up laundry, attempt to bring some order to the house that seems to have nothing to do with me. There is nothing to keep my mind from wandering back, always back…Grant starts crying, his morning nap over. I go to his room and lift him in my arms, holding his sweet, warm body close. The acrid smell of wet diapers hits my nose and I lay him down again to undress and bathe him. Then I put on his coolest summer outfit, swing him onto my shoulder and walk outside into the sunshine. I have promised the lady next door to attend a welcoming party, to visit with the women of the neighborhood. I wear my best, flowered cotton dress, glad to be able to fit into real clothes again, and slip on my high heels.

The ladies come out of the look-alike houses by the droves, walking down the street toward me. They coo over Grant and ask if I play Bridge.

"No," I answer, flinching at the thought. I'm not good at any card game, nor do I want to be. It's all those numbers, and the pressure to score…

As the coffee klatch breaks up I say my good-byes and carry Grant home, my heels clacking loudly on the pavement.

I close the door behind me and lock it.

◆   ◆   ◆

I meet Gloria for the first time at the market. She is a tired-looking young mother with three children in tow, two in the grocery cart and one hanging on to her left leg as she stops to talk to me. We exchange some light chatter about our babies, and how housebound we sometimes feel.

"Sometimes the only company I have is my piano," I blurt out.

"You must really love music," Gloria smiles. "But you need more company than that!"

"I know—I guess…" The memory of the neighborhood Bridge players intrudes darkly.

"I love music, too," she says. "I belong to a choir at church. Do you sing?"

"Yes—sometimes…" Wistfully I recall the Roger Wagner Chorale.

"Are you a soprano or alto?"

"Alto mostly."

"Our choir is desperate for an alto. We only have two. One lady just moved to San Francisco. Would you be interested in checking it out?"

"I'm…I'm not sure. It would depend on whether my husband would be willing to watch Grant. Which night do you rehearse?" Suddenly the impossibility of breaking away on both an evening and Sunday morning seems ridiculous. I know for certain Milt wouldn't want to come with me.

"Here's my phone number. I'd be glad to pick you up for rehearsals. Does your husband go to church?"

"No."

"What are you doing this afternoon?" she asks. Mentally I survey the empty day before me, the long weeks of empty days behind.

"Not much," I answer. "I just need to make dinner."

"Then come over for coffee. I live just two blocks from here."

"Right now?"

"Right now." She pulls her little boy's hands off of her skirt, quietly chides him for dragging at her, and grins up at me. "Come on. Just follow me in your car."

Gloria's house is a bedlam of toys, dirty laundry, and children's voices. Three children and one on the way. But she moves calmly through the disorder and interruptions, makes fresh coffee, then explains that she is right in the middle of her fifth month of morning sickness. "I still sing in the choir, though. It's good to get out of here for a few hours!" She eyes me over her mug. "I think you need to get out too." I feel like she is looking right through me. "I'll pick you up at 6:45."

The little Presbyterian Church where Louise and I had giggled, and Jenz and I had blushed at each other across the choir loft, was a dim memory from a time long lost past. I am a different person now. After one rehearsal at Gloria's church I know I don't fit in. I don't see Gloria again, although she calls often.

Homesickness presses in and I stay locked away. A deep gloom settles over my days. Everything I've known is gone. I sit at my piano and try to play. Sometimes I pound the keys, making Mendelssohn sound much louder than he intended, trying to tell the world out there who I am. Then I break down and sob because no one knows, not even Milt, though he hasn't done anything wrong. It's just that I feel as though my husband doesn't *see me* at all. And no matter how I try, I can't see him, either. The artist and the chemist. And yet...and yet, he is so handsome, so kind. Why the loneliness, the emptiness? Could simply moving away from familiar surroundings, from family, do all that? I feel inept, unsure—and how many times can I call Kirsten for advice on a recipe? I feel...rudderless.

And these feeling won't go away, I think helplessly, even now, so many months later. Regret is all I feel now, all the time. Was my astrological forecast right?

The thin Cottonwood trees in front of each house turn gold. In October Grant is six months old, wiggling and stretching and squealing with life.

The phone rings.

"Come down," my father orders. "Right away. Your sister is in the hospital. She's very sick."

"Is it—?"

His voice is flat. "Yes."

Milt's mother flies up to take care of Grant. "Don't worry about a thing. Stay as long as you need to." Her gentle kindness pulls me together as I pack.

◆   ◆   ◆

The hospital corridors seem so cold. When Grant was born in that same hospital I hadn't noticed what an ugly color of green the walls were. My father walks silently beside me, his face a frozen mask of apprehension. As we approach the room I don't know what to expect.

My eyes find her bed, then widen in horror at the unrecognizable figure lying there. I lurch past my brother and fall onto my knees by Kirsten's side. Her bony hand seeks my head where it is buried under the covers. I pull myself up and back away, taking a long look at the gray, hollow-eyed face that is my sister's. You were supposed to get married next month, I think wildly. You were supposed to be all well now. You told me you—you who thought it would never happen!—would be married in November! You and Bob! I swing around and see the man, who my father has finally admitted into her life, pressed against the back wall, tall and blond, eyes swollen with tears, hands balled fists at his sides. I look back at Kirsten. Her skin is stretched over eyes and mouth in a silent scream of unalleviated pain, and I watch her hands grope for the nurse's button, hunting erratically through the sheets toward the rail.

You are only thirty-four, how could I have not known? To have been so unaware, so stupid! Blindly I shift my blurred gaze to the window. My eyes fall on a stranger sitting in the corner of the room, wide, dark eyes on me.

"Who is *she?*" I blurt out.

"Her name is Kathy," my father says. "And she doesn't belong here!" He takes a long step forward and shouts at her. "Get out. Don't ever let me see you in here again!"

The tall, dark girl quietly gets up, looking deeply weary. She gives a last look at Kirsten, then walks past Bob, Dad and Erling. The look she lets fall on me is full of tenderness, holding my gaze. Then she's gone.

"She's been here day and night," Erling mutters. "A friend of Kirsten's from work."

"She never belonged here," Dad hisses through clenched teeth.

Time stands still as I kneel at Kirsten's bed. The voices of nurses fade into the background as I press my face on Kirsten's arm, lying inert on her tangled bedding. "Don't cry, Karin," I hear her plead softly. But I can't stop. As I rise to look at her through blurred eyes, a paroxysm of pain engulfs her face. Her arms arch up to seize the nurse's alarm buzzer, and in a small, strangled voice I hear plead, "Please, help! Oh, God!" I swing around, unable to look. I drop to my knees beside an empty orange plastic chair and cry aloud, "God, give her peace, please. Give her peace!"

Someone lifts me to my feet and helps me out. I find myself sitting numbly against a wall between Dad and Erling, staring into space.

Within a few minutes, a nurse comes and says quietly, "It's over."

It feels like I'm the one who ended it.

◆   ◆   ◆

Helena and Bill quietly let themselves in to our living room. She sits down on the couch next to me where I am slumped, eyes half closed. Her cigarette in its long holder hangs from her fingers, unlit. Dad paces the house, his face contorted. None of us speak.

Helena shifts restlessly, then gets up. She whispers to Bill, "Tell them I have to go home for something." Quietly she opens the door and is gone. A few minutes later the phone rings. "Karin," Helena says, "please come over here." I look toward Dad, wondering how I can leave him.

"Go ahead," Bill says. "I'll stay with him." Dad doesn't seem to know he is there or to see me when I leave. I push through the hedge and knock at Helena's door. It opens before I drop my hand.

"Come in," she says. "I have something to tell you." Her living room is dark, and she lights a match and holds it to a candle. "Sit down."

I choose the yellow brocade wingback chair next to the couch and stare at the picture on the wall of a Chinese cherry tree in full bloom. Helena lights her cigarette and takes a long pull, letting the smoke out in little wafts. The light from the candle plays on her wizened, kindly face, and a certain serenity gentles every fold and wrinkle around her eyes. She speaks.

"When I got here I didn't know what I'd find. I looked at the fireplace, fully expecting to see Kirsten standing by it." Kirsten used to love leaning by the fire, looking wistfully into the flames. She had once been in love with Helena's son, and they had spent many evenings together in this living room before he left and married someone else. It was because of me she couldn't go when he asked her. A wave of bitter remorse hits me. Why had she ever told me that?

Helena continues, her faced now furrowed with sorrow. "She wasn't here, of course, and I felt strangely disappointed." She took a deep breath. "Then I heard her speak to me, as clear as what I'm saying to you right now. She said, 'Tell Dad I'm fine. And that there's much more than he thinks.'"

I draw in my breath. I remember the table raising and the telepathy, but none of that matters. This feels real. This sounds like Kirsten.

"I'm telling you this, Karin, because it may be a long time before I can tell your father. Something may happen to me that I won't have a chance. And he might not accept it from me, anyway. You may have to tell him."

Dad and I have never talked about anything spiritual. I recoil at the thought of relaying such a message second-hand, and wonder for an instant why I hadn't been the one to hear it instead. As if Helena is reading my thoughts, she continues, "I suppose the reason I had to come home to hear her was because it's—well, it's *open* here, if you know what I mean, but it isn't at your house." I remember how terrified Dad had been by the table-lifting incident and how Kirsten had been merely bemused. Helena knows Dad almost as well as I do, I think. Maybe better. And she adores Kirsten; for years she has been her most trusted confidante.

"Tell Dad I'm fine. And that there's much more than he thinks."

My broken heart gives a leap of hope. Whatever it means, I believe it.

◆   ◆   ◆

Dad, Erling, and I drag ourselves out for dinner to a comfortable restaurant we had all frequented through the years. None of us have the heart to prepare meals; the familiar kitchen is a shambles of dirty coffee cups and spoiled food.

The bright-eyed waitress we've always liked refills our water glasses and pulls out her order pad. As she surveys the three of us she puts a hand on her hip and demands teasingly, "Well! Where's the *other* one?"

My father sags, his head bows slowly as he clenches his weary eyes against the tears that squeeze out onto his sunken cheeks. He stares blindly at the table. Slowly we all get up and leave.

Too soon it is Thanksgiving, with Christmas on its heels. The dreaded holiday spirit marches relentlessly toward us, and we cringe. Dad is silent, as good as dead except for his pain. We force ourselves through the motions of preparing meals and cleaning up. We spend long hours sitting silently in the dusk, no lights on.

It is hopeless to even think about re-enacting the Norwegian traditions Kirsten had unflaggingly performed every year I can remember. The buttery spritz rings, the tiny deep-fried cardamom flavored doughnuts, the cut-out Christmas *nissen* that draped the mantelpiece, the lavish yet artless positioning of candles and ivy and pine boughs. The smells of pork roast and red cabbage, the heavenly taste of caramel custard and real whipped cream…gone out of her hands forever.

I go back home to Milt and Grant before Christmas lands.

◆   ◆   ◆

The first leaves of early spring flutter on the slender trees across the street. Tender afternoon sun spills in the front window. Grant, almost a year old, has finally given up racing around on his newly found feet and succumbs to his afternoon nap.

I am dragging laundry off the line and piling it on the kitchen table when tears come suddenly and in torrents.

Kirsten taught me everything, and I didn't even know it! I couldn't wait to shed her, and she did everything for me!

I try to fold the stiff, clean sheet but find I can't do it alone, never have been able to do it well by myself, we'd always done it together before I moved away. I bury my head in its sweet, clean smell and weep until the sheet is wet through under my face.

She had taught me to chop parsley until it was fine as green dust. To stuff celery with cream cheese until it was flat and glossy as glass. She taught me how to make a centerpiece for the dining room table at Christmas, and patiently kept me at the job of polishing the silver candleholders, placing forks and knives correctly, and ironing napkins until every corner matched perfectly. She made sure I had clean underwear, woke me up every day, made sure I was ready for school, had something to eat...

God, I miss her so!

I relive that single hour in the hospital room over and over. No matter what else I am doing, I am still seeing my dying sister's hollow eyes and sunken cheeks.

A co-worker of Milt's is about to arrive for dinner and between my haunting flashbacks I have spent most of the day attempting to make an apple pie. Much of the five-pound bag of flour has ended up on the floor and all over me, and what I have vainly made into dough has landed in the waste basket. In desperation I dial the Economics Department at Berkley, begging someone there to explain why I can't make pie dough. The woman, probably a front office receptionist, is silent for a long minute, then says with a choking kind of laugh, "I don't think anyone here can help you, Ma'am."

When Milt sees me he groans and says, "You have to knead it, you know, like bread." He is determined to have apple pie for desert. He retrieves the last lump of dough and lunges into it, presses it together with all his might. At last it hangs together. I roll it out without a crack or tear, lay it smoothly into the pan, and bake it. He was right about the kneading part.

When it comes time to serve it, we can't slice it with the sharpest knife we have. "How about a chisel," Ron suggests. We all laugh, and dig into the apple filling. Pie, I muse, is one thing Kirsten didn't teach me.

I clean up the kitchen while Milt and his guest talk in the living room. When it is time for Ron to leave, he pokes his head around the corner and says, "Thanks for the great dinner." He adds, "I'll come back later for the rest of that pie."

"Why don't I just send it with you?" I smile. "I promise it won't fall apart."

There is a leftover fire still flickering in the fireplace, and I sink into the couch and stare into it.

Tell Dad I'm fine. And that there's much more than he thinks.

Milt is in the shower. I get up from the dying embers, my sister's words reverberating in my mind, and walk through the darkened house to the bedroom. I undress quietly and slip into bed beside Milt. A street lamp casts dim light through the curtains, and I can see his sleeping profile clearly. Milt, the handsome, brilliant scientist who made me his wife. Such a really good-hearted guy. But I wonder how long I can endure the loneliness.

It never occurs to me it is a loneliness self-created and self-imposed, a hiding place into which I am being drawn like a magnet to escape.

13

Word War

I storm out of the harmless-looking little white church and stride to the car with my teeth clenched. It has been nearly impossible for me to stay to the end, but I ball my fists tight in my lap and hold my breath until the last impassioned plea falls from the minister's lips.

Oh, the everlasting gall of that man! Why had I let that last call from Gloria impel me? "You need to get out and make friends," she had urged. "If you don't feel at home in my church, go check out another one." Feeling trapped and depressed, I venture out one Sunday morning about a month later. Milt doesn't object.

I park the car and step in from the garage, slamming the door. At the look on my face his brows rise up in question.

"Don't ask," I snap. Milt starts to give Grant to me, but I stop him. "Would you do me a favor and take care of Grant a little longer? I've got to write that man a letter right now. I'm going to tell that Bible-thumper what I think of all that hell and brimstone business he yelled about." I shut myself in the spare bedroom and sit down at the old typewriter.

"A message on salvation," I begin, "isn't worth much, it seems to me, unless there's some explanation regarding what one needs saving *from*."

A good beginning.

Suddenly my mind goes back to a long-forgotten incident. When I was fifteen a bright-eyed friend asked me if I was saved. I wanted to ask *"Saved from what?"* I didn't know I was in any danger, and wouldn't have believed it if told I was. So I had glibly answered yes. "But have you accepted Jesus Christ as your personal Savior?" she'd persisted. Visions of Christmas and Easter and Mrs. Cornwell's prayers and pictures of a sweet-faced shepherd with little white lambs had kicked in like a living collage. "Yes, of course," I had said, and it was a little like acknowledging that George Washington was the first president of the U.S. My friend had fled to her mother's room with the exciting news that I'd accepted Jesus, and I felt perplexed and embarrassed. Then I went home, not giving it another thought.

But as the months went on I visited her family almost as much as I did Meredeth; Lilly had become one of my best friends. But being at her house was unnerving. In this wealthy Christian home, the mother was an hysteric, panicky and shrill one minute, smothering and overindulgent the next. When Lilly's father came home they quarreled with each other in front of me. They all quarreled, loudly and with tears. I shuddered at being caught as an observer in this family's melodrama and was glad to go back to Meredeth's, relieved to be in familiar, if more esoteric, territory.

That memory is vivid as I dive back to my typewriter, trying to find the right words to express the disdain I am feeling toward church, Christians, the gospel of salvation, whatever that means, and all Christianity's hypocritical followers.

As I write, Jenz's last letter rises up to haunt me: "*You need to become a real Christian.*" The angry flame I began writing with flares even higher.

And I remember Kathy.

I type faster. Half an hour goes by. I dimly hear Grant whimpering behind the shut door. I rip page after page out of the typewriter, crumple them, and throw them in the wastebasket. Frustration grows along with my rage. Soon the wastebasket is full. Nearly two hours go by before Milt knocks on the door, asking if I am okay.

"No, just crazy," I say, "but come in anyway."

He looks at me questioningly.

"There just aren't enough words," I announce, exasperated, and tear the last piece of paper out of the typewriter. I take Grant from Milt's arms, and we relegate the little bald man in the pulpit to the place he'd yelled so loudly about. He never does get a letter.

14

Driven

Easter is ushered in under a grief that has deepened with every passing month. Milt eyes me suspiciously as my moods swing from the quiet tears of sorrow, to confusion and forgetfulness, to rage.

"What is happening to you?" he wants to know. He gets angry, too. "You might be becoming just like your mother!" That slices into me like a sword.

"It's just…I feel such remorse, Milt, that's the only word I can give you. It's with me all the time." I can tell none of this makes much sense to him, that he's had just about enough of it. "And I am desperate to see my father."

And it's true. Though I have experienced Dad's harshness, his rare humor, and his brokenness, tears that have been only for myself are now gathering for him. Is there any way I can go to him? Milt softens and considers it.

I have never driven any distance alone, but Milt can't take the time off from work to go with me. I beg him to let me drive Grant to Los Angeles over the Easter weekend. Even though he seems apprehensive, he finally agrees. "I really can do it," I assure him, hope welling up.

On the Thursday night before Easter he arranges the back seat of our '53 Chevy so Grant can use it as a combination bed and playpen, all padded up with pillows and flattened out with blankets. He gives me twenty dollars, quite enough for the round trip considering I will be staying at Dad's and eating out only once each way. I pack all of Grant's food, including the sterilized bottles of milk, which I wrap in newspaper and ice.

When I pull away from the curb early Friday morning I smile and wave at the image of Milt in the rear view mirror, watching us go.

The coastal road between San Francisco and Big Sur in early spring is breathtaking. I exult in my freedom, at the burst of energy and confidence I feel, at the contented sounds coming from Grant in the back seat, at the blue sky and sea on the horizon. The countryside is wild with fresh greenery, wildflowers spread out in joyous blue, yellow and pink carpets everywhere.

I pull into Carmel at noon for lunch and gasoline.

"Sorry, lady, gas station's closing."

"What?"

"Good Friday. We won't open again until three." He chuckles. "Everything's closed but churches."

Vaguely I remember something about a story I'd heard once: Jesus was crucified at noon and hung there for three hours while the earth shook and it got dark as night. But it never occurred to me that Good Friday was anything special where gas stations were concerned. Being stuck in Carmel for three perfectly sunny hours meant I wouldn't hit L.A. until well after dark.

"Maybe I'd better stay somewhere and continue on in the morning," I consider aloud.

"Ma'am, there won't be a motel between here and there that isn't full up," he warns. "Easter weekend, you know. Every room in this state's been reserved for weeks." I look at my gas gauge, near empty. Grant is crying, hungry, wet, and restless. I need a bathroom. When the attendant remarks that *everything* in town is closed except the churches, I believe him and don't look further.

We sit on the grass of a nearby park. I manage to feed and change Grant. I eat a jar of baby food. I keep shifting my legs under me, trying to hold it.

At last the gas pumps and rest rooms re-open. I make a dash; there are others in line before me. After the fill-up I have fifteen dollars left. Money is more limited than I realized. Definitely not enough to stay over somewhere and eat, too.

"Where is the next town south of here?" I ask the attendant, thinking about dinner.

"Next to nothing but cliffside switchbacks for the next hundred miles."

I get in the car and turn onto the road, not knowing what else to do. It is nearly four. We hit the famous Big Sur and its snaky road at dusk. The trees are dense on both sides, and as it meanders and switches back on itself, I glimpse how it flirts with sheer-drop ledges. My clammy hands grip the steering wheel so hard they hurt. Suddenly I hit an impenetrable bank of fog. Except for an occasional break where I can see cliffs rising to my left and ledges dropping down to the sea on my right, I can see nothing. The road curves endlessly as I crawl at ten miles an hour through one hairpin turn after another. Then the fog is compounded by darkness. I'm driving blind.

Finally, I spot lights and a group of buildings to the left. There appears to be a weathered old restaurant with a forbidding-looking hotel above it. Even so, it seems like an oasis to my tired mind. I pull into the parking lot, gather Grant and as much of our gear as I can carry, and get out of the car. I push my way through the front door and find myself in a Chinese restaurant. The rancid smell of deep-fried everything permeates the walls.

A small, elderly Chinese man leads me to a room at the top of the stairs. His eyes dart between my baby and me. The keys on his belt rattle as he unlocks the door. "Bathroom down hall. Is only one up here. You share."

I open the door to a closet-sized room, the bed filling all but a narrow walking space to a dirty sink in the corner. The mattress is bare except for a folded blanket. A ceiling bulb hangs down with a switch made of dirty string. The room is impregnated by the stench of grease and garlic. I want to turn and run, but I pay the waiting man seven dollars and close the door. I bite my lip, put down my suitcase and purse, and sink onto the sagging bed with Grant in my arms.

Grant's diaper needs changing. I offer him a bottle, but he is wide awake, round eyes eagerly exploring these unusual surroundings. Gingerly I board the smelly mattress, longing for sleep, but he crawls over me, refusing to stay by the wall where I repeatedly put him.

But now lights in my head are going on and off, and I can't control my arms. It comes on me so suddenly—the shadowy warnings—the aura—of a seizure. Exhaustion. I had forgotten about this inherited malady. The two episodes I'd suffered as a teen I'd filed away as insignificant. My arms flail, nearly crashing onto Grant's face. My eyes flutter and for an instant my senses blank out.

The full impact of what is happening tears at my chest. If I have a full grand mal seizure on top of Grant it could kill him! I gather him up, the head-lights still flashing, making me blink, and grab my purse and suitcase. Stumbling, I push through the door, tear down the stairway and approach the Oriental man at the desk.

"I need my money back." He stares at me as if I'd just spoken gibberish.

"I can't stay here!" I try to explain, but my mouth isn't working right. He turns away.

"No. You already use bed." he says flatly. "I keep money."

I begin to cry in earnest. "May I please use the phone to call my husband?"

I grip Grant in my arms as I try to explain to Milt all that has happened. There is a long pause. "I'm sorry, honey. There's nothing I can do." Another long pause. "You have the car, remember?" Of course, I know that. In the midst of this swirling haze, I feel stupid and embarrassed.

"You'll have to think of something." He hangs up. Coolly, I think.

I carry Grant and my luggage out into the cold night, nothing visible at all but the moist sheen on the hood of the car. Inside it feels colder yet, like closing ourselves in a refrigerator. I tumble Grant into the safety of the back seat where he will be safe from a seizure, if I were to have one. I sit there shivering, the lights in my brain still flashing, my eyes still blinking uncontrollably. The heater won't work.

For long minutes I sit slumped, alternately trembling then rigid with fright, tears blurring the dark pines smudged with fog. A heavy, clinging shroud of dread wraps itself around me, daring me to move. Slowly it dawns on me: I can't just sit here. Forcing myself to stay awake and do something seems safer than drifting off into a seizure, me unconscious in the front seat, Grant freezing in the back. I shake my head hard, willing it to clear, and start the car. Slowly I turn onto the twisty black road. Should I…can I…pray?

Desperately I realize that nothing I've ever thought *about* God is of any value. What I need is God Himself. But with the need comes the awareness of unbelief. There is a huge hollow space inside of me. I don't really believe in what I need. Is God real? Does He really *exist?* Even as I think it, I cry it out aloud. Into the black night I send up the challenge: "God! If you are up there, please help me!" The next words fall out of my mouth before my mind can think them. "If you'll just help me through this, I'll do anything you want, I'll give my whole life to you! Please—*lead me to a motel with a crib in it!*"

In an instant my world is altered. I am enveloped in peace, no longer afraid. I feel accompanied, even escorted. From above, behind, in front, all around, I sense an entourage, invisible to the eye, but more real than any other reality on this dark night. My driving feels disengaged; we are being driven.

Miles later, off to the right I see a long, low motel with a Vacancy sign. I stumble out of the car and into the brightly lit office. With a sense of wild hope, I tell the man behind the desk what I need. He looks at me with kind eyes.

"I think we might be able to help you," he smiles. He leads me to the only remaining room, the last one down the long outside corridor to the right. He turns the key in the lock, opens the door and switches on the light.

Quickly my eyes scan the room. There, against the wall to the left, it stands, white and clean, a baby blanket folded neatly over the side. *A crib.*

An astonished laugh escapes me, and I hug Grant to me in joy and relief.

In the silence of the long night that follows, under a canopy of calm where no seizure threatens, my heart swells and rises upward in continuous waves of thanksgiving. I stay on my knees by the clean-smelling single bed all night long.

"Thank you, God," I repeat over and over during the sweet, timeless hours. "Thank you, God."

He does exist. I am not alone.

15

Flight

From the start of my marriage to Milt I have shamelessly mourned Bill—and Jenz and Berni too. From which of these lost loves I have rebounded, cool-hearted, into Milt's arms I can't have said; perhaps, except for Berni, they were all rebounds. I only know I have to start over—again. If that means breaking promises, so be it.

Less than three years after our wedding, I pack as much of Grant's and my belongings that can fit into Meredeth's car, and leave him. She is happy to drive north to fetch me.

Well, they had warned me, hadn't they? Penn, who had my astrological chart drawn to the precise dimensions—latitude, longitude, hour (although that one was guesswork), day, month, year—of my birth, had predicted it: too-early marriage, early divorce. I feel totally exonerated.

I leave on the pretext of a temporary separation, and take Grant with me, of course. That is understood: mothers take their children. Meredeth is suddenly available to me again, urging me to be courageous. "Fly, my beautiful butterfly," she croons, all motherly sympathy and understanding.

I am not asking for anything but simple survival. The rest would come, perhaps, when my sign, Aries, would be in the ascendancy. For the moment it is enough for me to go back to the elements of life that I love and the community in which I can embrace them. Home, for me, is wherever I can easily get to UCLA, to the music department, the art shows, and to people whose bent is not quite so exclusively scientific. Meredeth walks me through all the legalities of divorce once she finally convinces me that it is the only reasonable answer to my ill-advised marriage.

"I'll get an appointment for you with my lawyer," she offers. "We'll take care of everything."

I am not surprised at how many things I can find to substantiate my decision. Others—Theo, Sekuris—are not only surprised but coldly outraged, although, oddly, not my father. "You never were happy," he says as I pour myself a cup of coffee in our old kitchen. "I knew you wouldn't be." I am dumbfounded by this bit of articulated, sympathetic insight coming from him.

Sophia is furious and won't speak to me. Louise, who has gone off to an expensive college, says little when I call her with the news. I hang up feeling like I have committed a crime. Divorce among the movie stars is tasty scandal; in the neighborhoods of 1959 it is simply contemptible. Louise and I lose touch altogether in the wake of my decision. Meredeth, however, is my ever-present ally as I make my plea of "irreconcilable differences."

There are few phone calls between us, and my heart is too hard to really hear any misery Milt might be experiencing at the loss of both wife and son. My mind is made up; I feel justified, especially when he doesn't contest any of it. I am awarded $250 per month child support, and I know that will have to cover everything, for I have no intention of working. After all, I have a toddler to take care of. Meredeth provides a bicycle with a basket on the front and a baby carrier on the back. I feel like I am under protective wings once again, yet free to fly my own way under Meredeth's covering. She invites me stay in her brother's old room in the Big House, since staying with Dad isn't an option. It is large and sunny, with a perfect corner by a window for Grant's little bed. Gisela still roams the house in a preoccupied, mumbling sort of way, but basically pays little attention to me. Of course Meredeth and Penn don't live there anymore, but they keep a close eye on us, visiting and picking up the old pattern of long weekends by her fireplace. But even there I feel the chilling absence of Kirsten and wonder what she would think if she could see me now.

Grant and I visit Dad as often as Meredeth can drive me there. Now that Grant is no longer an infant, Dad takes a bit more interest in him. But after the first few minutes of formal exchanges his eyes cloud over and his speech becomes brief and lifeless.

◆   ◆   ◆

Helena, happy as always to see me, beckons me to come over for tea. When I tell her that my marriage is over, she nods knowingly. It seems to me she always knows everything.

"I'm sorry for you," she says without judgment. "What will you do?"

I tell her about the $250 in child support. "I didn't ask for alimony. Meredeth is going to help me find an apartment in Westwood. We'll manage somehow."

Helena frowns slightly, then says, "You'll be all right." She pauses, putting a fresh cigarette in her long holder. "It's your father I'm worried about."

I know all the obvious reasons—the vacant listlessness, the pale, gaunt face, the hollow eyes, all fixed in a permanent, dark grief over Kirsten. I study my hands in my lap, wondering if there has been some new development, but not wanting to ask. There's already been so much.

"There are things you don't know about the house, Karin." I look up at her in surprise. "It's fully paid for, that's not the problem," she says quickly. "But it has to be sold, anyway."

"He hasn't said anything to *me* about that!"

"No, no, of course he wouldn't. He knows you're going through enough of your own troubles."

I stare hard through her front window. Limbs from the acacia tree next door are just within view. "Did you know the house is not in your father's name, but Kirsten's?"

"What? No. Why?"

"He wasn't a citizen when he came here. Non-citizens can't own property. So, because Kirsten *was* born here, the house was put in her name. She was twenty-one then." Tears begin to glisten in Helena's eyes. She lays her cigarette holder down on the ash tray and folds her long, work-worn fingers together.

"Kirsten died without a will," she is saying. "Do you have any idea what that means? Your dad would have to fight hard to inherit the house, and pay terrible taxes and legal fees. Even if he could afford that, there would be the complications of community property, since your mother and father are still legally married even though she's still in Norway. And still very ill. In her condition he just doesn't have the heart to involve her."

The words are a jumble of legalese to me; I can't make sense of them, but they resonate of something too unfair, too tragic to bear.

"What will he do?"

"The house is in probate now. After all the hospital expenses and probate fees, there won't be much left. He plans to send most of what it does bring to the state of Norway, since your mother has been cared for so long there."

Our sweet house! All the years of planting and weeding, of blooming acacia and clambering trumpet vine, of building trellises and training ivy to meander right into the kitchen…the swing that we never took down, the music, the piano! The way my father had sometimes listened carefully to my playing. The rare, treasured compliments when I played the *Moonlight Sonata* without a mistake.

The Christmases when he stood behind me and sang the Norwegian Christmas hymns in a voice husky with emotion.

I bury my face in my hands and cry out, "Why? Oh, Helena, why can't we keep it?"

"I know. It's hard to take in, isn't it? Legalities. Citizenship laws, community property laws. And Kirsten not leaving a will. Really, it's a terrible mess."

I look around the familiar living room of her house. Everything here is the same as it has been since I was a child, and right next door, the world has come to an end.

I realize with a sudden rending how much I want that house. Not just for my father, but ultimately for me, *for me and Grant*.

Dreams of the house, more poignant in the sense of its loss than any waking hours could endure, begin to haunt my sleep.

◆   ◆   ◆

Meredeth drives me all over Westwood Village, trying to find an apartment under $100 a month. It seems impossible. I love the tree-lined streets, the collegiate feel of the neighborhood. But two bedrooms for a single parent with a child? It will take a minor miracle.

Day after day we drive around, craning our necks for "Apt for Rent" signs. We are both tired and discouraged.

"Let's get out and walk a bit," Meredeth suggests. I agree gladly. Grant is getting fussy, and he needs to use his feet. I pull over and Meredeth lifts Grant out onto a wide, sun-dappled sidewalk. I stretch stiffly beneath a tall magnolia tree that spreads its branches across the windows of a shadowed two-story apartment building.

A slender woman with a child in tow appears, seemingly out of nowhere. "Are you looking for an apartment?" Before we can answer she goes on, "The one you are standing under is for rent—to someone who wouldn't mind cleaning it up. It's been vacant for quite a while because the owner doesn't have time to do it himself."

I look at Meredeth and whoop. She grins back. "How much?" we both ask at once.

"Ninety dollars a month. There's no deposit required. Just first and last. Would you like to see it?"

"Yes!" I swoop Grant up and wait for the woman to come back with the key. We sprint up the narrow stairs to the upper apartment. The lady opens the door wide and ushers us in.

I looked in disbelief at the mess inside and can't help but laugh; debris everywhere, filthy walls, shards of hastily removed carpet on the floor, nails sticking straight up from rotting wood lining the baseboards.

But there is no doubt in my mind. For outside the huge windows, filling every room with their beauty, are enormous magnolia trees in full blossom, and tall old pine trees, their feathery branches tickling the window screens in the breeze.

16

Unwelcome Revelations

With energy I don't know I have, I transform the abandoned apartment into a place of practical, simple beauty. While Meredeth watches Grant at the Big House, I pull up carpet nails, one at a time, cart out bag loads of debris, and scrub every wall and cabinet until my hands are raw. Thelma, the lady who had alerted me to the vacant apartment, turns out to be my next-door neighbor, a young mother with two small children. She often comes over to cheer me on, dragging her children behind her, and offers to keep Grant any time Meredeth can't. Meanwhile, I scrub. Soon the windows are sparkling, the old wood floor gleams, and a cheer goes up from my new acquaintances with every piece of furniture that comes in.

Pete, a district attorney who lives in the apartment behind mine, introduces me to a cadre of buddies he's invited to help me on moving day. I worry that they are working too hard on my behalf, but they assure me over and over that they are glad to help.

"Anything to help a little guy like him," a man named Greg says, "and...uh...his mother." I'm laughing when I spot Thelma hovering in the back-ground. "Why don't you send Grant over here," she calls. "I'll watch him for you until everything is in." When I hesitate, she says, "Come on. He can play with my kids. They need a change of faces. There's a sandbox out in back."

Grant, now a year and a half old, spends a lot of time next door. He is the buoyant center of attention among the other apartment mothers and their kids. And the moms are casual. No pressure to play Bridge. Our familiar furnishings in place, Grant quickly adapts to his new surroundings. His room is large, and there is a soft brightness in it that shimmers behind the magnolia leaves. The whole place feels like a tree house.

And so I call it: Our Tree House. I invite my new neighbors up to celebrate it, a housewarming party I throw myself, with coffee and pastries.

The bicycle Meredeth has provided is our only transportation, but my sense of adventure is equal to it. We ride to the local Safeway and jam all the necessities into the basket, then haul them up the long stairway piecemeal. Though we are confined within the limits of a tight budget I feel a soaring freedom.

◆   ◆   ◆

The sweet, mild summer turns to fall, and the days of single motherhood start becoming as heavy as the leaden skies bringing down the first rains. A slow-growing sorrow over the failure of my marriage doubles up with the grief of Kirsten's death and my father's tragic circumstances. My mood dips and rises precariously as Grant's curiosity and mobility increase. I become impatient, irritable. I am surprised—shocked, even—to find I possess a capacity for explosive anger, but there it is. If I frighten Grant with it, he doesn't show it. But he withdraws, seemingly placid, wide-eyed into the world of his toys.

Pete checks in on us often, bringing new playthings for Grant. And flowers for me.

Whenever I open the door to this big bear of a man, he brings with him a hearty cheer, and it pierces the darkness for a while.

I begin to let him draw out of me those things about my life that only Meredeth knows. There is a gentle courtesy in his listening. It would be easy to tell him everything, including my escapades in spiritualism with Meredeth and Penn, my lost love of their son, Bill, but I opt for caution.

He says he looks forward to meeting Meredeth. "I don't know, Pete," I warn him soberly. "She refers to herself as a 'white witch.'" As if on cue, Meredeth drops by the following Saturday while Pete is visiting me. Immediately I see something pass between them: two strangers making the usual conversational introductions, but who know from the first eye contact that they are adversaries. I am not really surprised; I have seen Meredeth's strong personality and charm intimidate or offend others, as if challenging them to a duel.

Pete, however, is not intimidated.

After a few high-pitched pleasantries she leaves with a flurry of gift-giving, bright good-byes to Grant, and a kiss on my cheek. I find myself sighing with relief when the door closes behind her.

"She's a powerful woman, isn't she?" Pete comments. "And just as beautiful as you said she was."

"Yes, she is very beautiful," I say, exhaling. I'm so glad he has acknowledged that. I dive in to defend her further. "She's really been like a mother to me, you know?"

"I can see that," he says. "Tell me more about her."

And so I do, starting with the Big House, the summers and weekends in that fabulous place where we cooked and ate and sang…and had séances. I brag about all the adventures we went on beyond this world, the ghosts Meredeth had seen roaming the halls, the astrological charts, the life readings, the spirit guides. I explain how my chart had warned against a too-early marriage, and how Meredeth and Penn had predicted my divorce. I tell him all about my past lives, the amazing way one had affected the next, how much sense it all makes. He listens intently, leaning forward in his chair as I map out each successive life Lotte Von Strahl had revealed to me, starting with my life in the Holy Land as a friend of Mary's. I feel oddly proud of my many pre-existences, in spite of that last one where, as a man, I had allegedly committed suicide.

Pete listens, studying my face as I elaborate on the details and answer his questions with quick answers. He must be a good D.A., I think; he's such a good listener. It must go with the territory.

Before we know it, dusk has settled in and my Tree House is darkening. "Time for dinner," Pete announces. "Where would you like to go?"

Surprised and relieved, I answer, "Anywhere we can find a high chair."

"Then let's go," he says. "I know just the place."

◆　　　◆　　　◆

I hear a ruckus on the stairs and a pounding on my door.

It isn't quite noon on a quiet Sunday. Pete has bounded up the stairs to invite Grant and me over to his apartment for lunch.

"Just got home from church," he says, panting. "I'll make pancakes and eggs for us all. My mother will be there too. She really wants to meet the beautiful blond in the front apartment."

"How nice," I reply, feeling slightly cautious about his reference to church. But I have been casting about for something to do now that Grant and I are up and dressed, maybe a walk down the block. I am feeling especially housebound and lonely, so I say yes. I wonder what his mother is like and feel a little shudder of fear. If she is anything like Lilly's mother…

We each take Grant by the hand and walk the short distance between hedges and up the stairs to his apartment. He opens the door and my eyes sweep the room from wall to wall. Nothing could have prepared me for the impact on all my senses as I cross the threshold from my world into his. The place is filled with the rugged, disorderly clutter of a typical bachelor pad. This is a man's place, no doubt about it. But as I am given the brief tour of this one-bedroom apartment, something else is meeting me. Books, everywhere. And every one of them is about God, in a sense I can only think of as 'religious'. These aren't the metaphysical books that occupy Meredeth's shelves, but Bibles, Bible commentaries, Bible dictionaries. Many of them in stacks, with the top-most open, marked, highlighted, and underlined, with scrawled notes in the margins. There are books on prayer, daily devotional readings, biographies about and autobiographies by "saints of the church," as Pete calls them.

As he moves through them to the kitchen where his mother is waiting to meet me, I sense a relationship between him and these books that is paramount, central, dominating. Everything Pete is, it seems, emanates from these books. All I have experienced of him so far is tied in some invisible, yet irrevocable, way to these books.

Pete's plump, soft mother, whose smile is just like his, gives me a tight hug.

"Oh, I've been looking forward to meeting you so much!" she exclaims, then dives down to grab up Grant. "You little cutie, you look just like your sweet mama!" she says with a chuckle, and ruffles his hair. I laugh at the term, "Mama", and wonder where she is from, she has such a sweet, lilting accent.

"I hear you're from Norway, Pete told me all about you," Dora says, as if she'd been reading my mind. "I'm from Missouri, myself, and so is Pete. I'm a widow lady, and aren't you just something." She smiles up at me with rapt admiration. "Just look at that pretty hair!" I blush and laugh. As if on cue, so does Grant.

Pancakes seem to make themselves between Pete and Dora, who both jump up to the stove in some long-practiced rotation, and we all talk at once, Grant included.

We are tired and full as we say goodbye to them and go back to our apartment for a Sunday afternoon nap. Now there, I think, climbing our dark stairs with sleepy Grant in my arms, is a man of real faith...whatever that may mean. I put him down and gently close the door; he is already asleep. I go to the kitchen to wash up our breakfast dishes.

Some of the titles of Pete's books had jumped out at me: *My Utmost for His Highest, The Screwtape Letters, The Greatest Story Ever Told.* I dimly recall a couple of those titles from my childhood. Some religious relative in Norway had sent me *My Utmost* when I was sixteen, but I'd never even opened it. I'd read *The*

Greatest Story while sick in bed with a cold; Mrs. Cornwell had given it to me. It had made me cry, but I can't remember why.

◆   ◆   ◆

Pete is now coming over to see Grant and me every day.

When I tell him my father has found an apartment a block away, he cheers. I don't quite understand the joy Pete gets out of that. Dad in an apartment! I wonder if he will expect me to visit every day. I agree it might be good for Grant to visit his grandfather. But what kind of grandfather could my reclusive old daddy be?

On a Saturday night Pete brings over all the makings for a spaghetti dinner. I'd had a particularly hard day with Grant, chasing, cajoling, fighting his terrible two-year old willfulness, and it is a relief to turn him over to Pete for a while.

Meredeth has dropped in earlier, leaving some books she's promised me. One is the story of Edgar Cayce, a man who has intrigued me for years, a spiritualist with astounding powers and out-of-this-world-and-time experiences. The other is by Annie Besant, who was a great medium with many past lifetimes to her credit. She was said to be full of cosmic wisdom. She is Penn's favorite writer.

I watch Pete as he looks through the books.

"What is your concept of God, Karin?" he asks.

His forthright question surprises me, and I struggle to answer. In my mind a picture of a twirling universe forms itself. Stars and moons and supernatural beings, spirit guides, a wild tumble of people born and dead and re-incarnated swirls through time without end.

"I don't know exactly," I answer. "Someone out there, somewhere. I mean, I believe He exists...but I don't believe the way religious people do."

"What do you mean?"

"Oh, you know. Churchy people." I blush, realizing that Pete is one of those. "I mean, the really narrow ones. The Bible being the only way, the ideas they have. That can't be it; it's too small."

Over dinner, we embark on a discussion that I suddenly have no patience for. I squirm as we work through the long strands of spaghetti and delicious sauce, and try to change the subject. "Oh, Grant," I coo at him, "Isn't this good? Pete makes really good spaghetti, doesn't he?"

But there is a quiet persistence in Pete tonight, and I can't escape it. Obviously we are far apart in our concept of God. I feel irritated and argumentative. I want Pete to go home. But he isn't moving.

"Do you pray, Karin?"

I want to respond hotly to his challenge, but I reign myself in, trying to disengage casually. Prayer! I remember Mrs. Cornwell's prayer over me. I remembered the Good Friday prayer I'd cried out on the road out of Carmel and…the crib. But that was different. Those prayers had been answered, I insist, by a God much bigger and more mysterious than any single book could contain. The Bible, for instance.

Pete smiles. "Do you still pray?"

"Of course I do," I snap, more sharply than intended. I want to bite my tongue. "But it's personal, private." Unwittingly I am repeating what I'd written to Jenz so long ago. My parting words to him, in fact.

Pete looks at me searchingly. For all his sweetness he irritates me terribly. He is trying to lead me down a road I have rejected long ago. Everything in me wants to combat his road, to wall myself away from his words, retreat back to the familiar freedom of the many roads Meredeth and Penn have taught me to explore, not his narrow one.

My mind feels dark, heavy. Actually, where is my spirit guide and all that promised supernatural help? What about all that piano stuff? I don't even have a piano anymore! And what lasting insight or explanation for things has my astrological chart ever delivered, anyway? It seemed so profound, so *true* at the time, but I can't remember anything. Except, of course, my divorce. Is it just fatigue, is it simply my imagination, or am I really drowning in a sea of confusion, my bravado melting like snowflakes in a desert? Because suddenly, that's how I feel. Something I have never felt before is creeping over me. I am deeply, terribly afraid—not of circumstances, or of single, nearly broke motherhood, or even of life itself—but of *myself.*

A recent memory of a conversation with Dad intrudes itself: with his ever present pipe in hand, he is shooting me a hard look and saying, "Don't ask me for any advice. You're on your own. You ought to know by now that life is just one big horrible joke."

◆   ◆   ◆

During the weeks that follow, I struggle through each day as though shackled to invisible weights. It is all I can do to keep up the apartment. I've never even been around two year olds, don't know what to expect. The order established when we first found the Tree House rapidly disintegrates: baby-food jars, dirty dishes, toys, unfolded laundry, and stacks of un-ironed clothes lie in heaps in every room. I need help, and there is no one. I need...

"The one you need is Jesus."

I hear it distinctly, as simple, impersonal, and concrete as the statement of a mathematical sum. It is spoken not by a voice, and yet by a voice, not by a thought of mine, and yet by a thought. In the middle of walking from one part of a room to another, like a radio turned on, then turned off. Strangely, I don't mull over it, because it disappears as quickly as it comes. When the "radio" stops, I keep walking, thinking my own dark thoughts, continuing to feel lost.

Another day, while putting on my clothes, and then while writing out a check, and again as I am picking up a toy, I hear it again. *"The one you need is Jesus."* Three times now. Still, I ignore it.

Pete brings over a ready-made steak dinner, complete with baked potato and salad. I want to tell him to go away and leave me alone, you are too happy and good, and I am too confused and tired.

But of course I don't. I can see that he is in love with me, and I can't just shut him out, not with all that food in his arms. And I've already kissed him plenty over the past few weeks.

After dinner, he offers to do the dishes but I say no. I gather the plates and carry them into the kitchen. As I rinse and stack them, Grant toddles around him, waiting to be picked up and twirled around. Pete lifts him up and swings him over his head, and both of them laugh. Grant still has that gasping laugh of a baby, and the sound of it melts and mellows me even on the hardest days. For a while Grant sits on his lap looking through a book, then before I know it, Pete has gotten him ready for bed. As I observe the two of them I marvel at their energy. I lean back on the couch and close my eyes, holding them still, hoping he will think I've fallen asleep and just tiptoe out.

He comes back from Grant's room and seats himself in the one easy chair. I feel like he is looking right through me.

"Karin," he says softly. "what do you want God to do for you?"

The question is too startling to allow irritation. My eyes flutter. "What do I want God to do for me?" A sly, warm light invades my shadowed mind for an instant, and I open my eyes wide. I am being invited to ask the great cosmic mystery to do something for me, something current, something beyond the faded image of the midnight crib on the Big Sur. The invitation is so fresh that I am oblivious to any memory of previous prayers. It is as though they had never been.

I rise up from the couch and pace from the living room to the kitchen and back, trying to think. I feel a little silly, like a little girl trying to make one wish over the candles on her birthday cake. Still…But this is, I remind myself, to be addressed to Pete's God. What would I like Him to do for me?

"To get rid of this terrible self-hatred!" In shock I clap my hand over my mouth, smothering a sob. What did I just say?

I am humiliated, and angry at being humiliated. I could ask God for anything, and this is what I speak out? Is it my soul that has spoken what my mind now wants fervently to deny? But I do deny it! I don't hate myself! Wasn't my contempt directed at others? Hadn't there been good reason for being critical, intolerant of all those who had made me feel like an outsider? Was that such a sin? What in the world has made me say *self*-hatred?

Pete is silent. He seems very far away, as though something huge is hanging between us. The room has darkened as the autumn light fails. But there is a different kind of darkness surrounding me, a whole houseful of it, a cavern with me trapped inside.

His far-away voice speaks, tenderly. "Then ask God for that. Ask him tonight, on your knees."

My mind churns like an engine without oil. "Okay," I whisper. I look toward the kitchen, full of dirty dishes. They're getting sticky now, spread all over the kitchen counter like flotsam on a beach.

"But remember to ask in Jesus' name."

At that, fresh anger flashes through the darkness between us. This is really too much. It's beginning to feel just like what Kirsten went through with her co-worker, Kathy. "Why?" I demand. The narrow provinciality of it! I have always prayed on my own, in my own name!

"Because," Pete responds evenly, "Jesus said, 'I am the way, and the truth, and the life; no one comes to the Father, but by Me.'"

The words sear my mind like a branding iron.

"How can that be!" I spit out. "What about the Buddhists and Hindus and all the rest? Doesn't God hear them?"

"He hears them," he replies. "And if they really seek God, not just religion, or religious practices to earn their way to Him, *they* hear *Him*. They recognize who He is." Pete sits quietly while I rail, not trying to stop me.

Finally, I am spent; there is nothing left to say except, "I need to do the dishes. You'd better leave." He gets up and offers to help, but I say in a cold whisper, "No. Please go now." He moves toward the door. "You might as well try it," he says softly. "You have nothing to lose." He searches my face. "You are a very unhappy woman."

The door closes gently behind him. The candles on the table have burned low, and I blow them out.

After washing up the dinner dishes, I turn off the kitchen light and make my way through the darkness to the bedroom. I take off my clothes slowly and pull my nightgown over my head. The street light beyond the magnolia tree casts leaf-shaped shadows on my bed. I sink down beside it and bury my face in the covers. My hand forms a fist, and I lift my head. I feel miserable and yet still cling to defiance, and I direct it all upward, through the ceiling, beyond the very roof above me.

"God. If what Jesus said about himself in the Bible is true—*show me*."

Then I remember what Pete had said. Numbly, barely above a whisper, I add, "In Jesus' name. Amen."

Sighing, I pull myself into my cold bed, drag the covers over me, and fall immediately to sleep.

17

Nothing But the Truth

The room is too bright.

So bright I awake suddenly, as shockingly as if there has been an earthquake. The autumn sunrise is more brilliant than any I have ever seen. Blindingly bright…and yet, my eyes are wide open. I sit bolt upright, staring into the white light, emblazoned by it and shaken to the core.

The light is, beyond question, *Jesus.*

Tears gush from my eyes like a fountain. The salty streams wash debate clean out of me. I stare at the One I've ridiculed and scoffed, who now stands before me. The world falls away.

His face shows inexpressible joy, as if He's been waiting for eons outside the walls of my room, my heart, my mind, for just this moment. I am undone, unmade.

"At last!" The words come from Him as a joyous, relieved cry from a heart in pure, perpetual laughter, eyes searching mine in penetrating love. His countenance displays fulfillment of a longing since before time…for *me.*

I don't know how long Jesus drenches me in the cleansing wonder of His presence. Theory is swallowed by Fact, doubt melts in the heat of His perfect Light. All I've ever wondered, fought to defend, believed, thought I knew, drops away as if of no consequence, discarded without reproach by the hand of Truth Himself. All that remains inside of me is the startling freedom of humiliation and surrender.

At some point, while the tears still shoot from my eyes like joyous geysers, I jump from my bed and run to the telephone.

"Pete," I choke out the words, "It's true. It's true!"

I hear him take in a shuddering breath.

"Of course," he says.

Quietly we weep together.

18

Fellowship in the Spirit

I often wonder why such an encounter was granted me; one that would forever sweep away any doubt that Jesus Christ was and is and forever will be the Son of God, born, crucified, resurrected and here. Lord of the earth yet at the same time Creator of the universe. I always come to the same simple answer: because I needed it. I needed Him, face to face. The years of spiritualism in all its forms had taken me far from the kingdom of God, had thrown long shadows over my mind and soul. I was desperately lost, more lost than I knew, without Him. The corruption I was becoming, and would ultimately not have recognized as myself, needed a crisis rescue. A saving. His life for mine.

During those first blissful days, I had no idea what demons I would struggle to conquer, often failing, along the way. But knowing Him changed everything in the time it takes to think a thought. He was the fact around which everything past, present, and future must revolve or go madly out of orbit.

Those first weeks, I felt attended by Christ's living presence with every step I took. He was never out of my thoughts because He was palpably never out of my reach. The Light was necessarily turned low so that ordinary daylight and star-light once again took their place, but the fact of His holy Personhood never diminished. There was no heaviness about that companionship, no blinding glory, no sudden religious piety, no compulsion to beat my breast with moans of *mea culpa, mea culpa*. His kindness would lead to repentance of staggering dimensions—later.

Sometimes I giggled to myself at the sheer joy and astonishment of Him, but the laughter *started* with Him. This reconciliation was joy begun in Him and transmuted to me. There was nothing I did that wasn't initiated by Him. He whom I had never known I now loved, because He had shown me His love for me was real—reality itself—and always had been.

Pete came over with a present. I opened the small box and could not have been more awed at his gift of a Bible had there been diamonds in it. He had written an inscription on its first page:

Ask, and it will be given you;
seek, and you will find;
knock, and it will be opened to you.
For every one who asks receives,
and he who seeks finds,
and to him who knocks it will be opened.
Matthew 7:7-8

I had asked, sought, knocked. I recalled with a certain shock my clenched fist, my loveless demand, *"Show me!"* Somehow I was assured my posture had not shocked Him. Not only did He answer and give and open, He set about a work in me that would fulfill my request to "get rid of this terrible self-hatred". I had no idea what I was in for, or how long it would take. I was re-born, embarking on a new life centered on God in place of self. The first step would require looking at the root of that instinctual self-hatred, confess its reality, and be dismayed, with groans that came from the deepest pit in me. The process of facing evils of pride, fear, self-pity, and lovelessness would continue for the rest of my life, a journey of mountain tops where one could see forever, and deep, dark valleys where the way was sometimes indiscernible.

But at last I knew what I had been saved from, what being *saved* meant! Myself—caught and blinded by the same powers of darkness Jesus had faced off on the cross and triumphed over on my behalf.

◆   ◆   ◆

Pete took me to church with him, and at first I was scared to death. Every preconceived notion I'd developed about Christians rose up in a wall of resistance. Christ, I knew now, was reality…but Christians?

The animated talk as they gathered in groups before and after the service, the unbelievable friendliness; it couldn't be real, could it? Did they all really enjoy each other that much? I insisted on sitting in the back row so I could get out without getting caught in one of their huddles.

One Sunday a girl strode toward me. I'd noticed her laughing the loudest and shining the brightest within a little knot of people before church.

Suddenly I realized I'd seen her before, while working in the chemistry library at UCLA. She was the grad student everyone had disliked, made fun of, rejected as a loser. Three years ago Barbara had been forbidding, cold, hostile to everyone, thundering up and down the halls between the chemistry lab and classes with her head down, mouth frowning. She had reminded me of those pictures of an angry Beethoven. But this woman coming toward me was walking tall, eyes sparkling with intelligence and warmth.

"How great to see you," she said, and extended her arms to embrace me. "Meet me for lunch after church and I'll tell you my amazing story." I was dazzled by her changed appearance. She grinned. "I know. I even look different."

Pete invited Barbara and me to join him and other UCLA students after church. "We usually go to the local Hamburger Hamlet on Sundays," he smiled. "They know we're coming." I was cordially introduced to the mix of undergrads, grad students, and professors that made up this astonishing group.

"A highchair for the youngest student here, please," Pete called out, riding Grant on his shoulders. We squeezed into the largest booth and soon the restaurant was filled with the explosive laughter of this unselfconscious crowd. Over several cups of coffee I learned that Barbara was in the last stages of getting her Ph.D. in chemistry.

"Just one more oral exam and I'm in," she said. She remembered Milt well, and remarked, "He was brilliant. Gave me a bad time like everybody else, but God knows I deserved it. I wasn't a very nice person B.C."

Barbara had, like me, been personally encountered by the living Christ. For her, it was just as she was about to commit suicide.

"I was married to a guy I really loved," she told me. "Then one day he announced he was a homosexual and didn't want to be married anymore." I shuddered. "It didn't go over with me too well," she went on with a dry little laugh. "I decided to check out." I listened to her without blinking as she continued. "I had all the pills I needed, the glass of water, the works. I had a fistful of the pills ready to pop in my mouth when I looked up...and there He was." Her face took on a soft glow. "Apparently He had other ideas." She looked up at me. "Funny, isn't it, how we both know we were met by the same God? Jesus." Then she added, "There really is no other."

"No question," I answered.

"No question at all," she replied.

Barbara and I became, against all odds, the best of friends, bonded together beyond and in spite of educational and intellectual differences. Bonded in Christ, the great equalizer. Over and over I asked her to tell me the details of her story; over and over it filled me with the affirming *Yes* of my own experience and the settled peace that came with it.

That peculiar joy—of hearing other's encounters with the Living Christ—was unlike any happiness or pleasure I'd ever experienced before, and was to become the hallmark of my new life in Christ.

At the first service one Sunday, Louis H. Evans, Jr., the minister of Bel Air Presbyterian Church, invited anyone who wanted to dedicate their lives to Jesus to meet with him after the service. Instead of sliding out the back door unseen, I pushed my way to the front, almost afraid I wouldn't get there in time, to give him my commitment. He met me with a grin of joy and an enveloping embrace. "Welcome, welcome," he murmured. "Welcome to the Kingdom of your Father."

Immediately thereafter I felt an insistent desire to be baptized, even though I had been christened in the Lutheran church in Norway. "You were baptized as a baby," Louie Evans explained. "We don't re-baptize in our church."

But I wasn't going to be put off. For weeks I hounded the handsome young minister, showing up in his office between services. "I really need this, Louie," I kept saying. Finally he smiled and said, "This must be of God. Next Sunday prepare to be baptized." Then he added, "You'll be the only one. Are you comfortable with that?"

"Absolutely," I replied. My heart was satisfied and I looked forward to that day as if it were my wedding day.

As I knelt before Reverend Evans, so tall and strong, robed in his black ministerial gown, a full congregation behind me and a large choir in the loft before me, he laid his hand firmly on my head and quoted from Paul's second letter to the Corinthians: *"Therefore, if anyone is in Christ, he is a new creation; the old has passed away, behold, the new has come. All this is from God, who through Christ reconciled us to himself and gave us the ministry of reconciliation; that is, in Christ God was reconciling the world to himself, not counting their trespasses against them…"* Then he cupped his hand under a tilted jug of water and let it flow from the top of my head down my neck. Deep, warm chills flowed through me. Warm and powerful, from head to toe and back up again. A shower bath.

"I baptize you in the name of the Father, the Son, and the Holy Spirit."

I was riveted by a wash of glory and love so profound that once again the tears fell in a torrent. I knew, as I was bent nearly double at Louie's feet, that this was my wedding day. The Son of God, Jesus the Bridegroom claiming His bride, betrothing me to Himself until that time when he would come for me.

When I stood up and smiled into Reverend Evans' shining face, the water he'd sprinkled on my head gently running down to my shoulders, I knew that the most important transaction of my life had been made. "The old has passed away, behold, the new has come." I had left one world for another, the one dark and chaotic, the other glowing with revealing light.

I sat quietly in the front row for the remainder of the service and let the glory continue to envelop and infuse me. When the congregation filed out and the choir members made their way down from their loft, I shook myself out of my ecstasy and, feeling a little drunk, joined those emptying the church.

I was stopped. "Karin!" Three choir members rushed to me with eyes wide. "There was light! We all saw it, all around you! You have been *blessed*!" I nodded through tears. I knew that! But whatever had happened on the outside, for anyone to see, was nothing to what was going on inside. I didn't question it then, just bathed in it. But later I found myself wondering again, *why*? Why me, and not all—*all* the others who come to Him in the same abject neediness? Signs and wonders, light and glory, faces illuminated, miracles performed? It wasn't long before I found out I was only one of millions through the ages who had been encountered by the living Christ, face to face in a bedroom, or motel room, or heart to heart in a desert across the world, or in a car on the freeway during rush hour. And always for the purpose of making the truth of Him known to others, for telling the life-saving, soul-saving story.

His story.

Through long seasons of stupefied groping to align myself with my Father—to desire His will only to fail to do it—I would need that special encounter with Him as a living memorial of His absolute, unwavering love for me—and for all those traveling with me, swimming against the world's current, striving against its winds, navigating in the power of the Holy Spirit this amazing life on this beautiful, mysterious, besieged planet.

19

Old Suitors

Meredeth looked bemused as I reported the glorious thing that had happened to me. She shook off her sweater and went to the kitchen to put on a pot of coffee. Grant, dragging his blanket, followed her.

"Well, that's wonderful. Are you actually going to church?" Her face was clouded.

"Yes! And it's wonderful." I showed her the Bible Pete had given me. I opened it and read the inscription.

"Hmm. Yes. How true." She abruptly changed the subject. "Karin, come with me to a friend's house tonight. You'll be my special guest. There's a man there I want you to meet, a true trance medium. He's absolutely fascinating." She looked at me brightly, waiting for a reply.

"Okay, I guess so. When do I have to be ready? I'll have to get a baby-sitter." The words came out before I could call them back.

"Oh, I've arranged all that. Grant can stay at the Big House while we're gone. Gisela and Karl are there, and so is my brother. He'll be fine with them for a couple of hours. I don't want you to miss this."

The destination was a large home in Coldwater Canyon, a wealthy neighborhood peopled by lawyers and doctors and other rich professionals. "Many of the guests are from the Beverly Hills Episcopal Church," Meredeth informed me. "Some of them you've met at the Big House when Gisela did a brunch. You'll remember them."

Church people. This should be interesting.

As we stepped into the large living room I saw about fifty people seated in church-like rows, waiting expectantly for the middle-aged man before them to begin the proceedings. We were ushered to two seats that had been saved for us in the middle.

"His name is McGaffey," Meredeth whispered. "He's waiting for his spirit guide to take over his voice. He'll be in a complete trance soon." There was subdued whispering and coughing among the visitors.

I squirmed as I noticed what he was doing to prepare. He was belching. Long, loud, and without any sign of embarrassment. One after the other, resonant burps rang through the room as he paced, seemingly oblivious to his audience.

"What in the world is he doing?" I asked.

Meredeth patted my arm. "He has to do that to clear the way for the spirit to enter. It won't take long."

A torturous half-hour later the belching stopped. With eyes closed he sat on his stool and appeared to be sleeping. A little later he began to speak. The voice was distinctly different from the one he'd used to welcome us. I watched and listened, wide eyed.

One after another the guests questioned the spirit about what it was like on "the other side," and asked if he could he tell them the truth about death and dying. Was there really a hell?

"No, no," the spirit answered, "God is not like that. It's all love and acceptance for everyone no matter who you are or where you are in your karmic evolution. Hell is a myth developed by the early church fathers."

Were friends and relatives there? And if you can find them, what are they doing? And—where *is* God, actually? The questions were edged with emotion that I recognized as fear, doubt, anxiety. All coming from people who were supposedly churched.

Something I had never felt before within this old, familiar context began to rise in me. Revulsion. Disgust. Impatience. I wanted to stand up and shout, "Fools! Why are you eating up what this creep is saying? Why are you turning to this nobody when you could go straight to the top for your answers? To God Himself, to the Lord! This pathetic medium won't tell you the truth about life here *or* on the 'other side.'" But of course, I kept quiet.

But rage continued to build in me at the unholy absurdity of this meeting, and without a word I got out of my seat, threaded my way past indignant stares, and walked out the front door.

I got in Meredeth's car and waited for nearly an hour. I could hardly wait to get away from that fancy house and all those super-educated, rich people who were burning with an unquenchable thirst for whatever a "spirit" could give them. It made me feel sick. I suddenly understood what the word 'abomination' meant—something unacceptable to God; a lie. And for the first time I felt fury at the Liar. For I had come to realize he, too, was a real entity.

Such a short time ago, I had been one of them. A victim, just like they were. Pretending their spiritual eyes were fully open when they were drugged, half-closed.

When Meredeth finally arrived, we didn't speak. I saw her shadowed eyes, her clouded expression. I knew she was ashamed and embarrassed at me. But looking at her as she put the car in gear, backed out of her parking spot under a magnificent oak, and crunched gravel swinging onto Benedict Canyon Road, it wasn't just that she was displeased with me. She wore none of the brightness I'd worshiped in the past. Her countenance had shrunk; she looked worn out. I couldn't wait to get home, away from her, away from the clinging darkness I didn't want to be part of any more. If she had ever been a mother figure to me, she was dissolved as of that day.

20

Over All the Power of the Enemy

Helena called and invited me to dinner. Bill had died suddenly a few months before, and Helena's hand shook as she inserted her first after-dinner cigarette into its long holder. She had begun to suffer from emphysema, but that didn't stop her from smoking.

"I've been having some pretty terrible experiences," she began. "Now that Bill is gone I realize how much I really loved him." Tears swam in her eyes. "We were married for forty years, and in all that time I resented him because he wasn't the one I had wanted to marry. Now I realize how precious he was to me."

I sat in silence. I thought about the long years of separate bedrooms, the deliberate distancing that kept them apart. Now, Helena seemed totally alone. Whatever spiritual adventures she had had in her private world had become meaningless. Kirsten was gone, Mrs. Cornwell was gone, Bill was gone. All to a place where she couldn't reach them.

Helena knew I was going to church, but she didn't have much to say about my announcement that I was a Christian. She frowned slightly and said somberly, "Well, dear, I hope you find what you're looking for."

"I am, Helena. I am."

Some months later I visited her again. She still lived in the house next to the acacia tree. Now, in February, it was in full, pungent bloom with the fuzzy yellow flowers I loved so much. She had picked up Grant and me in her old Chevy station wagon and made a small Indian curry for us to enjoy. Grant loved it, especially the peanuts and coconut.

"You won't believe what happened to me last week," she said. "I've never been so frightened in my life." It was hard for me to imagine the cool, collected Helena frightened by anything.

"I woke up in the middle of the night last Monday, and there, on the end of my bed, was a cobra, coiled up and looking right at me."

"My God," I breathed.

"It was real, no doubt about that," she asserted. "I could feel it with my feet. I could almost smell it. Then, in the space of a few minutes, it vanished." She drew in a wheezy breath and coughed. "I could see where it had been; there was a hollow in the quilt."

"What did you do?" I wondered if she was losing her mind.

"There was nothing to do," she answered. "The thing was gone. But I was terrified and didn't sleep the rest of the night, I can tell you that."

I shuddered.

"But that's not the end of it," Helena went on, grinding out her cigarette. "It happened again the next night, and the night after that." She looked steadily at me. "Three nights in a row."

Now I was really frightened for her.

"I could have reached down and touched it, Karin. It was as real as you are, and it stayed longer and moved closer to me each night. I was practically paralyzed with fear.

"The next day—just two days ago—I was so desperate I called a couple I'd met in the flower shop. They live in the San Fernando Valley and claim to be Christians. Something just told me to call them, I didn't know where else to turn. I knew they were strong in their faith." Helena pulled at her dead cigarette and reached in her purse for a replacement. "You won't believe what they told me to do."

"What?"

"They said, 'The next time it happens, speak to it and say *In the name of Jesus, be gone!*'"

"Did it happen again?"

"The very next night. It was horrifying beyond words. It crawled toward me. I could barely get the words out at first, then I found myself shouting at it, 'In the name of Jesus be gone!'"

"Did it go away?"

"Yes! Just like that. I could still see the path where it had been on the quilt, but it disappeared instantly." She gave a wan smile. "It hasn't been back. And it won't." She looked steadily at me and said quietly, "I think we're onto something, dear."

"What do you mean?"

"Demons. Demonic spirits. I know that now without a doubt. What I saw, what scared the life out of me, was just that." She looked up at me, her eyes crinkling in a tired smile. "We've been taken for quite a ride." From one world to another, I thought. Two worlds. The world we see…and the one we don't—usually. But every bit as real. The true, and the deception. One offering life, the other threatening horror and death.

She breathed deeply, her breath ending with a cough.

I opened my Bible randomly. I found myself in the Old Testament, in the book of Deuteronomy, chapter 18, verses ten through fourteen:

> *There shall not be found among you anyone who practices*
> *divination, a soothsayer, or an augur, or a sorcerer, or a*
> *charmer, or a medium, or a wizard, or a necromancer.*
> *For whoever does these things is an abomination to*
> *The Lord; and because of these abominable practices the*
> *Lord your God is driving them out before you. You shall*
> *be blameless before the Lord your God. For these nations*
> *which you are about to dispossess, give heed to soothsayers*
> *and to diviners; but as for you, the Lord your God has not allowed*
> *you so to do.*

As I read, a dark veil that had surrounded my thinking fell away. My lust for the occult was taken from me completely. I was free.

Now I could look with clear eyes at the terrible thicket of false hopes Meredeth and Penn—and dear Helena—were caught in. Every astrological prophesy, every word from every séance, marched before my eyes, and I perceived the lie, catching a grizzly glimpse of the Liar. For only the hellish things predicted had ever come to pass, none of the prosperity and power and riches…or love.

I thought about the way Meredeth and Penn had gloated over Gisela's chart, seeing the way her timely death might give them wealth. Gisela had indeed died, lonely and abandoned to her tortured mind, but there was no money. Karl had also died. Meredeth and Penn were scraping to get by. The Big House was empty and for sale.

Meredeth ultimately left Penn for another man. I felt heartsick at this news. In time that man left Meredeth and went back to the wife he had left in his lust for Meredeth. "I guess that just wasn't meant to work out," Meredeth said lightly.

Following all that, Meredeth moved to a tiny apartment in Orange County, alone. I visited her there and bragged that I was free of all the travels into the occult she had led me through. Even as I said this, I saw a challenge in her eyes, and something inside prompted me to regret my braggadocio.

For in truth there was one last stronghold that had been left unassaulted, and it was a snare that caught me blindsided.

21

Pilgrim's Regress

I hardly knew it, but I was still enthralled with the concept of reincarnation. My haphazard wanderings in the Bible hadn't unearthed anything to change my mind about it. It still made some comforting sense to me as I looked around at a world of impossible inequities.

My new Christian friends kept warning me that such conjectures were out of bounds, but the words Lotte Von Strahl had given me stuck like darts in my soul. I still craved that particular form of fatalism and the self-justification it afforded. And I still didn't quite understand how Jesus' death on the cross fit into the picture.

"How about some coffee, darling?" Meredeth had fixed her best California salad and *linzertorte* in honor of my visit. "Are you enjoying having your own car?" I nodded. My father had given me his old Mercury when he upgraded to an almost equally old Mercedes.

Meredeth and I ate and chatted, but I felt a strain between us. The old spark of mystery and adventure was gone. She no longer smiled as she used to. And I didn't hang onto her every word about life and love. Actually, she wasn't saying much about all that now, anyway.

We went into her living room and I curled up on her couch with my coffee. She sat cross-legged on the floor.

"I've been learning how to do life readings," she announced. "I'm not very good at it yet, but I'd like to try with you. Are you game?"

Unbidden, the old curiosity rose like a thirst. Without thinking I agreed.

"Lie on the floor and close your eyes," she commanded. I did, stretching out and folding my hands over my stomach like a corpse. I waited, trying to let myself drift wherever she bid me to go.

"Now, you are going to go into a trance." I felt a sudden uneasiness but pushed it aside. Quietly she began subtle suggestions, advising me to describe whatever came to my mind. I drifted, and pictures undulated before my mind. "Go with them," she urged. "Tell me what you see."

A cliff. An ocean behind me. A house on a hill. Long ago…so very long ago. Was it an island?

"Crete," Meredeth exclaimed. "A thousand years ago. Go on!" Her voice became hard, sharp. "Go into the house, tell me what you see." I obeyed, her words too strong to resist. The entrance way, steep steps, dead bodies laid out in rooms as in ancient times. A plague? Awful, grizzly—death everywhere! "It's your family, Karin, the one you had when you—"

I shook my head, my body felt like it was shrinking inside my skin. I couldn't hear what Meredeth was saying but her voice had become a high-pitched shriek. I jumped up and shook myself hard. "No," I cried. "No more. I have to leave. This is bad." I wanted to add *evil* and *a lie*, but I could only think of fleeing. Meredeth stared at me, her face ashen, her dark eyes wide like great hollows in her blanched face.

"I…I'm sorry, Meredeth, but I've got to go." I grabbed my jacket and purse and ran out the door with a mumbled good-bye. It wasn't a parting, it was an escape.

Shaking, I got in my car and began the long drive home. My mind felt scrambled, fear flared like fire in my throat as I changed lanes, watched exit signs, nearly missed a truck's front fender as it roared down on me. What had I been thinking to go back to the old chaos? The old deadly darkness? Fool! I didn't belong in that world anymore, and I was no longer allowed there. I had been saved from it!

I prayed, I called out the name of Jesus, and found strength. *"I am the Way."*

I repeated His name over and over, and drove home on it like a road.

◆   ◆   ◆

"Go to the book of Hebrews," Barbara suggested when I told her of my ghastly experience with Meredeth. "It's in the New Testament, near the back." She gave me a hug and shook her head sadly. "You'll find what you're looking for there."

I opened it and right then and there, and after long shuffling of pages, my eyes fell on a verse that cut through like a sword. Hebrews 9:27: *"—It is appointed for men to die once, and after that comes judgment."*

One life, one death. One lifetime to perceive and learn Christ Jesus and His redeeming love—or not. To understand our pitiful, orphaned neediness, and search for and accept that reconciliation—or not. To come to grips with our sin, and receive His forgiveness—or not. To come to the source of that forgiveness, His cross, His death for us in our place—or not. He, ever available to the hungry heart everywhere on the face of the earth, through all of time, by means of a preacher, a dream, a missionary, a Christmas carol, an encounter with the Holy Spirit during illness or sleep...He searches out the heart's cry to be met *in this one life*. No spiritual evolution through epochs of time, no earning heaven or paying to avoid hell. No climbing an endless ladder to perfection, only to slip backward to start again. Only by faith, only by the humiliations of life and the humility of dying to the phantasms of human pride in all its forms. No paying by karmas without number.

I felt like I was standing naked on a rock, divested of all the colorful clothing Lotte Von Strahl had dressed me up in. Layer after layer came off and fell in heaps around my feet, washed into the sea around me. I was *one* soul, living *one* life, without excuse, without the means to earn my place in heaven. I only had to open my hands to receive it, to take my place beside my Bridegroom. He had taken death and hell for me and was now alive—life itself—in me forever. *Jesus.*

22

Full Circle

Helena was the only one of the old neighbors and friends with whom I remained close until her death. When she reached her seventies I watched her go through what I went through before that autumn morning when Jesus woke me from sleep. She struggled with questions: Was the Bible really the revealed Word of God? Was Jesus truly the only way to the Father? When Jesus said, "I and the Father are one," did He really mean it in the explicitly exclusive sense it seemed? She had a lot of Hindu in her soul. She wrestled with the many roads to God, the many lords and gods that seemed so perfectly benign. Yet, as her emphysema (she never did stop smoking) got worse and her clutch on life began to slip, she was seized with a holy fear about the eternal life that loomed ahead. The encounter with the demonic had deeply frightened her, and the release she had experienced when she commanded them "to be gone in the name of Jesus" could not be ignored. She finally told me she had surrendered her battle into God's hands and confessed her faith in Jesus as the Son of God. She exchanged the many voices, with their claims and demands, for the One Voice, and finally joined the same Presbyterian Church Jenz and I had sung in so many years before. She died shortly thereafter. Her wise old Methodist missionary father was surely on heaven's shore to meet and embrace her.

Through the years Ilse Braandt had generously sent letters, illustrated with her own fine watercolor paintings, keeping me up to date on her boys. Jenz followed in his sea-captain father's footsteps and joined the Merchant Marines. He and his wife settled in Nova Scotia. Berni? He had completed his schooling in Germany, married a fellow lab student, and became a professor at Heidelberg University. I felt a twinge of jealousy, then smiling resignation. I would never have made a good lab partner in ornithology.

Penn died alone in a tiny apartment in Santa Monica, penniless. Meredeth attended him lovingly to the end. She told me this during her last visit to me while unloading electronic gadgets for Grant, now twelve, to enjoy.

"And," she said, "I am attending a Bible study, learning about Paul." I let the statement drop into silence. She didn't offer more, and I was too stunned to ask. I never saw her again after that, but hoped…and prayed.

Pete? He walked straight ahead in his walk with the Lord, and married a woman who loved him.

◆   ◆   ◆

About three years after Kirsten's death I got a phone call from Kathy, the girl who had kept unwelcome vigil by Kirsten's bed in the hospital for nearly a week before my father threw her out. I gave a shout and leaped for joy.

"I secretly kept track of you through the people at Rand Corp.," she admitted. "I've prayed for you every day. I hope you're not offended."

"Offended? I should say not! I want to see you. There's so much to tell you, to thank you for." Kathy seemed surprised, and then put in, "I have some things to tell you too. Are you free this afternoon?"

My little apartment had become a meeting place for many young Christians from UCLA who talked and prayed with me as I took my baby steps with Jesus. Barbara and I sat for hours reading *C.S. Lewis' Screwtape Letters* and *Mere Christianity* aloud to each other. Søren Kierkegaard gave us food for thought, along with George McDonald and G.K. Chesterton. Pete came up the dingy steps often and found us engrossed in the Bible and other books, all laid out open on the floor, and seeing he couldn't get our attention soon left with a chuckle. Even Rosie Greer (how he found out about this fledging believer I can't remember) came to see me from time to time.

But no visit excited me more than the one Kathy was about to pay.

I hugged the tall, dark-haired Swedish girl hard when she came through the door.

"I'm so glad I found you," Kathy said over her coffee. "You've been on my heart for a long time." I smiled at her and urged her to continue. I thought of the enemies she'd made—even my sister—as she boldly professed Jesus the Savior to her coworkers. She had unflinchingly spoken up in His name no matter what the backlash. She reminded me of John the Baptist.

"I want to tell you about your sister," she began bluntly.

The mood was instantly somber. I put down my coffee cup and leaned forward, hugging my knees to my chest, and felt my heart pound hard against them.

"When I met Kirsten at Rand Corp., I just fell in love with her. She was beautiful in a quiet, self-possessed way. And she was so gifted in her art." Kathy closed her eyes for a moment, remembering. "When I found out she had cancer I prayed for her constantly. I couldn't get her off my mind. Kirsten wouldn't talk about it." How well I remembered her stoicism. After her death, going through her things, I came across the truth about her silent suffering. It was all there on a dog-eared calendar, each day crossed off over brief, penciled statements of anguish. Monday, October 3: *When will this agony end?* Tuesday, October 4: *I don't think I can take much more.*

"Then I heard she'd been rushed to the hospital," Kathy went on. "I asked to take a week off from work so I could be with her as much as possible. Your dad didn't like that much." She smiled ruefully. "But I knew it was an assignment from God." Kathy looked up at me, assessing my reaction.

I nodded at her, smiling. "It's all right, Kathy. You can tell me everything. I'm a believer now too."

Her face broke into radiant joy, and she laughed aloud. "Oh, thank you, God! I've been praying for you all this time. I was pretty nervous about what you would think of my barging into your life." I gathered her in another long, silent hug. Releasing her I gave her a level look. "You are—and have been—an angel."

She shook her head. "Oh, no. Just a hard-headed Swede." We both laughed at that, and I replied, "I think we hard-headed Norwegians could give you a run for your money. But please, go on."

Kathy told me how she had camped out in Kirsten's hospital room, day and night, for nearly a week, fasting the whole time. She had prayed over Kirsten when she was asleep and talked to her about Jesus when she was awake. She'd encountered lots of resistance. Kirsten kept saying, "It's so hard to believe. I've seen so much…you can't just force that on somebody." How well I remembered my own arrogant resistance, and how ludicrous it now seemed. Why was it so hard to surrender to unconditional love?

"She told me she had made a confession of faith in Jesus during some youth rally in Norway when she was a young teen," Kathy continued, "but then life had gotten hard, and she became bitter. The day you came—the day your father made me leave and she died—I went home to get some sleep, planning on coming back that evening no matter what your father said. I prayed that the Lord would wake me up the minute I was needed, then fell into a deep sleep. At 2:10 I woke up as if I'd been shaken. I was totally aware that God was with me, and that Kirsten was with Jesus."

I felt the familiar wash of sweet chills run over me.

"I prayed for a while," Kathy continued, "Then I picked up the phone and called the hospital. Kirsten had died at exactly 2:10."

We were both silent for a long time, heads bowed.

"By the way," she said finally. "I'm on my way to see your dad."

◆   ◆   ◆

My father visited Grant and me often. His apartment in Westwood Village was roomy and pleasant, but he complained that it cost too much. It was still difficult to be with him. In the wake of my conversion he played the sardonic adversary.

"All your prayers answered, eh?" He scoffed. "Well. I guess if you pray hard enough anything can happen. But it never worked for me." I wanted to counter him, explain that it wasn't how hard we pray—but I stalled. It was impertinent to argue with the seventy-five years of his tragic history. So I reverted to playing the quiet, polite daughter, a role I had learned well.

The only time I broke with this pattern was when he returned from Paris and his work on *The Longest Day*. He had been there for over six months, often sick. "The rich food nearly killed me," he remarked. "I even had to give up cream in my coffee."

I hated to broach the subject, but decided to dive in. "Did you go up to Norway to see Mother?"

"No. I couldn't go back." He swirled his drink, clinking the ice. "You never can, you know."

"You mean, you were a stone's throw away from where you were born, and you didn't go?" I suddenly felt fierce with reproach. "How could you do that, Dad? How could you not go to see your wife?" I was up from my chair, looking down on him, seething. "*Didn't you love her at all?*"

I had never seen him shrink. But there he sat, almost swallowed by the chair he had dominated, he and that pipe, for all the years I could remember. His face was pale, cheeks hollow beneath bones that suddenly looked so fragile. His eyes, red-rimmed, shrunken, looked up at me as if he'd been whipped, pleading for me to stop.

"No," he whispered. "I loved her too much."

There was nothing I could say. I whirled around and left, shutting the door cleanly behind me. Then I cried.

A few weeks later he appeared at my apartment door. He had regained his composure, standing as tall as his stooped shoulders would allow as I offered him a cup of coffee. That done, I sat down and steeled myself for the usual long, uncompanionable silence.

This time, there was no silence. Gripping his pipe and avoiding my eyes, he cleared his throat and announced that he would pay for me to go to Norway.

"You need to do it," he said flatly. "It's time you met your mother."

23

Reunion

Even as I experience getting off the train from Oslo to Asker on a clear, shyly warm May day, I try to imagine describing it to someone else: I am walking up a path through pale green, gracefully drooping willow trees, edged by masses of early spring wild flowers, now stepping onto the grounds of what looks like a country estate set within acres of lawns with budding gardens surrounding a white stone mansion which is, in fact, a madhouse...

How will I ever describe later what it feels like walking into that building, standing in the spacious, sun-drenched foyer...then glancing at the winding staircase to the upper stories, and seeing on every landing, leaning over banisters, women of every age gaping at me with eyes wide and wild, as if I were either the ugliest or most evil being they'd ever seen?

I walk slowly up the stairs, knowing I have to get to the third floor, because that's where I am told I will find my mother. One by one the women shrink back in what appears to be a mix of fear and loathing as I approach. Somehow I know they too have been waiting for my arrival, like some strange celebrity they can't make sense of.

I tell myself it is only just that—what *appears* to be—because they are in their own world and don't see *me* at all. Isn't that what Kirsten taught me so many years ago when I had asked so many unanswerable questions about Mother's condition?

The hammering of my heart slows, my breathing calms, and I push my way through the arms that both reach out and recoil at my approach. I smile at the faces. And as I go I speak the name of Jesus aloud. *Jesus.*

By the time I arrive at the third floor I am calm, cool as if encased in a layer of spring snow. A nurse with short brown hair and pale blue eyes meets me in the waiting room. She extends her hand with a bright smile and beckons me to accompany her to a large ward down the hall.

"We're so happy to see you here, Karin," she says. "Your mother is doing so well just now, and has been waiting for you for a very long time." I feel a stab of guilt, as if I've been deliberately late by several years, but the nurse is chattering on warmly as if she has known me all my life. In a way, maybe she has. "You've had quite a homecoming, I hear. How lovely for you. Now you have another homecoming, to your mother who talks about you all the time and loves you so much." I wonder vaguely how the nurse would know this, then remember the many woven table runners I have received from Mother's hand these past few years. She has not been idle here, but has kept her hands busy with handwork that is truly the work of an artist.

The nurse opens the door to the ward and ushers me in. There are several rows of beds against pristine white walls. Flowered curtains drape the tall windows. A dark haired woman sits slouched on the bed closest to the door, a pink blanket scrunched up in her lap, her hands kneading it like bread. She stares at me vacantly as I walk by.

"Inger!" the nurse calls out. A fragile looking blond woman in her late sixties rises from a bed in the far corner and comes forward slowly. She is wringing her hands nervously. She is wearing a dark blue wool skirt and a white embroidered blouse under a drooping tan cardigan. Her eyes search my face from behind thick glasses, and between flickering smiles she chews on her lip. Her teeth are yellow and glitter with gold fillings.

"Karin, this is your mother. Inger, your daughter—at last!" Heartily the nurse brings us together in an embrace, then chirps, "Follow me into the sun room. The cooks have made special pastries for the occasion, and you can sit there and get acquainted for as long as you like."

Who is this woman, this one I am to call Mother, whose anxious blue eyes regard me questioningly? What can I say to pierce that veil of unknowing between us?

Involuntarily I glance at my watch. Two-thirty. The train won't be returning for Oslo until four. An hour and a half…

I throw myself into high-pitched light chatter, as if she might be somewhat deaf, and frantically attempt to pick subjects that won't refer to either my father, my dead sister, or my recent divorce. I needn't have worried so much about words. My mother sits mostly silent, listening to me, watching me.

Over the next weeks there are many such visits. They are always the same, except for one where Onkel Anders fetches Inger in his little Fiat to spend a whole day with them at the comforting gray house on the hill. Maybe he senses my trips to her are draining me. I can't help but notice that Dagny and Anders are welcoming and courteous to Inger in a detached kind of way, going about their own business without joining us at the table spread out in the garden. Dagny, being Dad's sister, probably has many unpleasant memories of Inger's breakdown and the agony he experienced at the expense of the whole family so many years before. I wonder if that is the reason for her diffidence. Nevertheless, courtesy rules. Dagny has prepared the usual mid-afternoon smorgasbord in the dining room for later, but has also laid a fresh pot of coffee with an array of pastries out on the lawn table. Now that it is June the warmth makes being outdoors under the cherry tree mandatory. I am learning how passionately the Norwegians value their long summer days.

I wonder if this is the first such visit with Inger since Kirsten came to visit in '53. Dagny edges away quickly once Inger and I are settled outside under a shaft of sunlight. I pour the coffee and bite into a *kringle* as light as air, glad to have something to do with my hands. I am safe here, and feel relief at being able to connect with the clear-eyed faces of Anders and handsome, grown-up Bjørn, who are working on the flowered borders in the yard. It is heaven just to hear the snatches of the normal conversation drifting through the sweet air. So often, the intensity of Mother's anxious countenance overwhelms me.

I didn't expect to have these feelings. But in fact I have been more than overwhelmed these past weeks. With each trip to the hospital I experience an increasingly alarming pattern: I know I have no choice about going; I *must* go. I force myself onto the train, and studiously seek solace in the blossoming countryside during the two hour ride. I always arrive to the same scene as the first. Grimacing or vacant faces of women staring after me, followed by lengthy, strained conversations with Mother, who, when she speaks, is unnervingly precise in her American, no accent at all. While at the hospital I feel the cool, composed part of myself take over, as if I am blessedly anesthetized from the appalling reality of the broken lives around me. But then—the trip home. I slump in my seat on the train and feel a darkness, liquid as an ocean of black ink surround and seep into my being. The landscape out of the train window looks menacing. Though the train is crowded I feel isolated and alone. I stare sightlessly out the window. The barrenness without and within looks like the North Pole from the plane during the trip over. There's a brooding bleakness in the world that whispers to me that there's no use, there's no use in anything. I find myself wringing my own hands. When I arrive home, I shut the bedroom door and rock myself on my bed, clutching my Bible to my chest. What is happening to me? And will it happen the same way next time?

I shake myself out of my memories of these awful journeys and look up to see Mother staring at me over her coffee cup. I blink and tilt my head away from her gaze. It is good to feel the sun blazing through the cherry tree behind us.

Bjørn breaks the mood by wheeling two-year old Grant into the yard on a red wagon. When he stops near Inger's chair, Grant attempts to get up but he tumbles out instead, hitting his head on the stones. Inger gasps and puts down her coffee with a clatter.

"Oh, no," she cries, clutching her fists to her face. "Oh, no!"

Grant picks himself up with a grin and climbs back into the wagon. "It's all right, Mother," I say quickly. "Mother! He's not hurt, he's fine!" But with a stab of annoyance I can see my reassurances are falling on deaf ears. Inger's eyes continue to stare in alarm at her small grandchild once again seated happily in his wagon.

"Oh, no," Inger repeats over and over. Her eyes are wide above her hands clenched against her chin. "No, no, oh no."

Grant is lost in a happy vortex of attention from aunts and uncles, so if he minds my absences I'm not aware of it. When I come back from the hospital visits I gather myself together for meals, for walks with Grant to a nearby park that is, in fact, a cemetery. I learn enough Norwegian jargon to make people laugh, take up smoking and knitting to be companionable. Dagny and Bjørn's wife form the nucleus of a kind of women's knitting circle every afternoon over coffee and pastries. Neighbors stop in and treat me with lavish cheer. Everyone is unfailingly kind and gentle. I try to act normal, to hide the turmoil that is brewing beneath my bright smiles.

But normal no longer feels normal. I feel like one under water struggling for air. No one seems to notice. "You're so very like your mother," my sister had often said. What if that is true? The thought of being with—but especially being like—Inger, her eyes darting, her lips chewing each other, her hands twisting—fills me with loathing. I want to run away.

◆   ◆   ◆

"Please, have a seat," Dr. Ormstadt says. "Here is a little bouquet of peonies your mother picked from the garden herself; they just started blooming a few days ago…here, my dear, take them." He smiles a thin, tight smile as he waits for me to respond.

I take the bouquet and sit down in the low chair in front of his big mahogany desk. I murmur "Thank you," and with that he embarks on a brisk conversation about the virtues of this aged facility, how many fine people he has had the privilege to treat here, how many have stayed quite comfortably for several years.

"Did you know that your mother has been one of the worst cases of schizophrenia in this hospital? There are so many different forms of this disease, you know, we are only beginning to recognize its patterns, much less know the exact correct treatment." He pauses, finger tips together, musing. "Yes, it's been a long road for Inger. And," he looks meaningfully at me, "such a disease can happen to anyone. *To anyone.* She comes from a strongly religious family, and it seems that in the face of this mystery she has been—perhaps—misunderstood. So many are."

I am sitting still as a rock as Dr. Ormstadt continues.

"But your mother is doing very well now, has been for many months. We believe the current treatments are working wonders. She's so well, in fact, that there really is no reason for her to remain here. That is what I wanted to talk with you about." He looks like he's about to lean forward but changes his mind and sits back instead, eyeing me intently.

A shock wave like ice water washes over me. Am I hearing right? Dr. Ormstadt hurries on. "You know she's been here for twenty-two years, a very lengthy stay, and has received the most excellent treatment. The newest drugs the psychiatric profession have to offer proved successful in her case. She's perfectly well now, you see. We would like her to return to America with you."

"But—Oh, I'm so sorry—but that would be impossible!" I cry. "I am divorced, with a young son—I hardly know her—!"

"So young to be divorced," the doctor says. "I wonder, what on earth could have happened to make you do that, with such a young child on your hands?"

Furiously I search for an answer to that impertinent question. Am I really required to lay out the details of my failed marriage to this man I've never met before? Doctor Ormstadt takes his cue from my flustered silence and interjects: "Well, you are her daughter, a grown woman. Surely you could make provisions? You have an apartment, I suppose?"

"Of course I have an apartment, just big enough for us. Grant and me—"

"What about your—ah—father? Doesn't he live quite near you? Couldn't he help? I see here—" He pauses, frowning, flips through some papers on a clipboard and begins again. My heart is hammering against my ears. "I see here they are not divorced, but legally separated—that he only left her here because of the war. Really, Karin, the state cannot continue indefinitely with one who has recovered…"

I lurch up from my chair, gather my purse and coat, and hurl the bouquet of peonies onto his desk.

"Doctor Ormstadt, there is no way in the world I am in a position to bring my mother home to the United States with me. The idea is impossible, out of the question. My father is—" Words choke in my throat at the thought of my father's outrage, his horror that this has been put before me, before *us*. For it would be us, of course, my father and me, taking in this stranger. He—reconciled with her—in my apartment? Or would it be his? His small, shabbily furnished bachelor—or more appropriately—his *widower*—apartment floats before my imagination. My mother, there, with him. But no! Because yes, he's a widower, for hasn't he always lived as though Mother were dead?

"My father is definitely not in that position either," I say, my voice shaking. "He's an old man now. They have been separated for over twenty-two years, he never even *speaks* of her…!" Tears sting and I know I am babbling now. The doctor cuts me off sharply.

"All right, all right my dear. But it is what your mother—it is what we *all*—want. I do not see why, as her daughter, her *grown* daughter, you cannot…"

His words fade out behind me as I flee the room. This, I vow as I tear down the stairs past the usual gallery of staring eyes, will be my last visit to the sanitarium at Asker.

But of course it won't be. Or…should I just—run away? Tell Onkel Anders and Tante Dagny I need to go home?

In my room that night I press my face deep into my pillow and wrestle with the dread I've come to recognize. It feels like poison is seeping through the walls of the room. Is God really in this with me? Is he with those poor souls, including Mother, in that prison fashioned after a castle they call a hospital? Does anybody ever really leave there, hearts alive, minds renewed? If so, how? After twenty, thirty years…childhood, youth, marriage and parenting…have all been lost? How utterly cruel! How incomprehensibly pointless!

The doctor's words, "It can happen to anyone," echo in my mind, and I press my face deeper into the pillow and my hands against my ears. I am faced with a sickening certainty: I do not love, do not want, cannot understand or cope with my mother and her life-stealing illness. Worst of all, I am afraid of her, as if she is contagious.

The cemetery is not far from Onkel Anders' house, and I walk there under a cold rain. It is June now, but settled warmth has not yet come to Norway's southern coast. The trees drip, the fog smudges the landscape, and I am reminded of Edgar Allen Poe's dark, menacing moods that cling and can't be cast off. Claps of thunder bring down a fresh downpour but I push on through the cemetery's wooded paths.

As I trudge blindly around headstones, I am remembering the last time I'd visited Mother during the second week in May.

We had sat outdoors, in the beautiful rose garden behind the hospital, with the usual coffee and small cakes on the table between us. The sun had been unusually bright and warm, but we were comfortably shaded by a great old tree whose branches were beginning to bud with spring blossoms.

Mother was calm that day, with none of the lip-chewing or hand wringing that I had come to expect. She wore a flowered summer dress and though her face was heavily lined, her graying blond hair was shiny in the sun and neatly styled, giving her an almost youthful look. She even had lipstick on. Her speech seemed particularly fluent and relaxed. This, I thought, must be how that officious Doctor Ormstadt often saw her, the one who had tried, to my horror, to convince me she was well enough to leave the hospital and come home to California with me. He must have seen her only on "those lucid times" Kirsten had told me about so long ago.

Sensing an opening between our minds that had been closed up until then, I had ventured to ask questions about her life—the life she had lived *before* I was born. I poured her more coffee and she cradled the cup in her lap. Her eyes sparkled and she opened up as easily, as casually as an experienced swimmer dives in the water and begins the crawl. What a change! I didn't want to waste this time being surprised, so I followed each answer with more questions. Her responses were quiet and measured.

"Yes, we lived in the heart of Beverly Hills," she said, eyes shining. "We had a little dog. We walked him down those wide sidewalks under those glorious Palm trees, with Kirsten and Erling tagging along. We had lots of parties. Beverly Hills, as you must know, is practically summer all year long." She laughed. "Some of our parties were pretty wild, I must say, and we took many of them to our cabin in Tehachapi. Those were prohibition days, you know, and your father and his cronies were good at making home-brewed liquor."

My father—the rebel against prohibition. A true Scandinavian! With a small smile I remembered my father's story about the snakes, the real snakes which he had thought were a figment of too much of that liquor, but were actually draped over the fence in front of the Tehachapi cabin, shedding their skins right there as they did each year. He had scared himself witless, thinking he'd gotten the D.T.s. That was one story he liked to repeat, if begged hard enough.

"Did a lot of you go together?" I asked, my eyes on Mother's face. "Did you have couple-friends you did things with?"

I knew I was moving into dangerous territory, but an urgency drove me. What little I knew about my mother was second-hand; now I wanted to hear everything I could from the woman herself.

Mother didn't seem perturbed. "Oh, yes, we were a real mob. Usually about six of us, sometimes eight. All young, good-looking men and women with whom we were friends, mostly British and Norwegian transplants. They traveled back and forth from Europe to America just like we did."

Mother was quiet, remembering. Then, as if I wasn't there, she said in a flat voice as if to no one: "Women. There were always other women."

I held my breath, startled at Mother's sudden coolness, waiting for what might come next. It was as if her countenance were coming from a different personality altogether than the one I had been meeting with for weeks. I leaned forward and waited, my fingers twined tightly together in my lap.

Mother waved her hand dismissively as she continued. "That's just the way things were then, in the early years—the twenties, the thirties. Men always had other women, right in front of their wives. Your father was a ladies' man like all the rest."

"Why? Why was it like that?" I pressed, knowing as soon as it was out of my mouth that it was an irrelevant, silly question.

"Too many babies. I didn't want any more babies. That's what happened with all the wives. It was too hard. So—I denied him."

This ancient reason for adultery had never occurred to me and I couldn't hide the shock in my face. I was out of touch with history. I was living in the gleeful promiscuity of the sixties, in the brave new world of birth control. Of freedom from the fear of pregnancy, in marriage or out.

I waited for more, because I knew there was more. Kirsten had hinted at it once.

"Once I went to visit him on the set of one of the movies he was working on in England. He was there for several months at a time. I had been staying in Norway at that time with Kirsten and Erling." Mother looked down at her lap. A breeze lifted the blossoms draped on slender branches gently around her. "I found a letter in his jacket pocket. It was from a French woman." She looked up and gazed steadily somewhere beyond my shoulder. "The woman's name was—oh, I don't remember. Nikkie, I think. The letter was quite hysterical. She said she was pregnant, and that if he was not willing to take care of her and the child she would throw herself off a bridge."

Mother hugged her chest and settled low in the chair, pushing her legs out straight in front of her. "In the same pocket there was another envelope, addressed to her in his handwriting. He hadn't mailed it yet, obviously, and of course he was going to, but I opened it anyway." She paused, her eyes half closed, as if reliving a scene in every detail. "He wasn't going to help her in any way."

There was no hint of bitterness in her voice, only what seemed like perfect, detached recall, without emotion.

I was unwilling to let it—the *emotionlessness*—remain. My own body was taut with it, ripples of feeling surging into my throat. Would my mother let me in? *Please God, let me get in there!*

Impulsively I asked, very low, "Did you ever forgive him, *Mør*?" It was the first time I had felt moved to use that endearing term for *mother*.

Mother's eyes took on a strange, faraway glint.

"Forgive him?"

"Yes. You know. For what he did—to the other woman. And to your marriage. To *you*."

The very air changed. A shadow fell over the table.

My mother's low answer was raspy, as dry as a dead leaf falling on other dead leaves.

"Forgive him for what?"

She hesitated for a split second, as if weighing the thought. She turned her head away and the light lay on her profile in sharp shards against the gathering shadows of late afternoon. Then she turned to me and said lightly, "There's nothing to forgive."

My mind exploded in disbelief. A horrible realization oozed in to take its place. In that moment—the moment of the lie—I saw the real woman disappear behind the Liar who had taken over her soul. The liar that had real, supernatural substance, expression—and worse, control. I wanted to slice through it with a sword. Of course there was something to forgive! There was *everything* to forgive! Betrayed love was at the very heart of the world's need for forgiveness. It was that which had led Christ to the cross...to die ten thousand-times-ten thousand deaths for the treason of the world's unfaithfulness. Why did denial always have to get in the way of healing? Did I dare try to break through it—on His behalf? On hers?

"Do you believe in Jesus, Mother?" I asked. My tone was stronger than I had dared to hope, even though it trembled.

"Believe? Believe what?"

"In Christ? In Jesus—as Savior? You used to go to church…" Now my heart was pounding so hard my voice sounded far away, as if reverberating out of a well. A glint I had seen in my mother's eyes faded into nothingness, a blank, like shades drawn on a window. She shifted slightly in her seat, picked at a crumb on her dress.

Coldly she answered, "You mean religion? Christianity?" She shrugged, and glanced absently up to watch a cloud drifting over the sun.

I watched her, motionless.

"I can take it or leave it."

I quicken my step as I approach the cemetery under the pouring rain. I am quickly soaked to the skin. Tears are pouring freely too, and I think again how like a scene from Edgar Allen Poe this is. This is not just a cemetery, it is a graveyard; underneath my feet are tombs, and the whole place is haunted with despair.

There is no one else in the park on this dark day. I huddle under a dripping tree. It's time to let the dreaded fear, the whole, hideous question free.

"Lord!" I cry aloud, half choking on my tears. "What guarantee is there that I too won't lose my mind? Just like Mother? *What guarantee is there?*" I'm on the ground, rocking back and forth on the wet grass, hugging myself. I am drenched through, my hair plastered in soggy ribbons to my head. I scan the sky, searching. Dark, billowing clouds, deep gray from one end of the earth to the other. Skies in Norway seem so high, so much bigger and wider then anywhere else…

Then I see it. Something—a *word*—filling that high, wide, gray sky. An invisible banner with a word as big as the universe behind the clouds. From east to west it hangs like a rainbow, soundless yet louder than any word I've ever heard.

"FORGIVE."

Then the addendum, as close as my ear: *"Forgiveness is the key to sanity. Forgive your mother as I have forgiven you."*

It took years to face how deeply fear of my mother and her illness had lain dormant in me. Irrational, yes, but real with its own power to sicken and distort. When I returned to America, to my lovely Tree House, I felt, as well as knew, that I had abandoned her, run away, just as I had wanted to do, and felt deeply guilty. I had cut short my stay with my baffled aunt and uncle. A black depression was sucking me downward and I needed to get away before it brought the whole sweet house down with it. In a very real way, what I had feared had come upon me, though in a different form from my mother's. Depression held me in its grip for many months following my return home.

The little Bible Pete had given me was the only source of peace during that time. I read and reread its promises. Jesus spoke clearly. *"I will never leave you or forsake you."* I had every reason to believe Him. He who had met me in my unbelief would meet me in my faith, however young and fragile. And He did.

Mother wrote to me often, letters full of pity and self-recrimination. Many letters stayed unopened on my bureau for weeks. I wasn't yet strong enough to meet her in her pain. How to answer? What to say? I continued to ask Christ to slice open my cowardice, expose it to the light of his love, and to heal me of it.

Gradually the shadows melted away. I could open her letters and reply with bits and pieces of our lives, Grant's growth and play, my applying for a job and landing it. Little things. It was possible to be in the safety of a detached place and yet to connect. It was possible to send her my love. It was even possible, for brief, shining moments, to *feel* that love. I learned to pray for my mother, an authentic reaching out to her from the heart. That's when I let God override my instincts to run and hide from what I would never comprehend, the *why* of the torments of mental illness. Prayer cut through where feelings couldn't go.

In my quest for understanding I never got far from God's answer to me in the cemetery on that rainy day in June, the day of Poe and despair. *Forgive*, he said. *Forgiveness is the key to sanity.* Certainly he was speaking, not just in the universal, urgent terms so often found in Scripture, which apply to all people at all times, but to me. *My* sanity. *My* need to forgive, my need to plead for forgiveness. That, surely, would be the central thread of truth that would weave itself through all the remaining years of my life.

Even as I grew in my walk with Christ, I continued to harbor many conflicted and disturbing feelings in relationship to my mother's illness. Her passing from sanity to "a world of her own" affected all of us with ongoing, covert grief—not the clean grief due to a death, but the baffled, guilt-ridden grief of losing a beloved wife's and mother's mind to schizophrenia. Was my father to blame, as some of Mother's relatives insisted? Adultery can break a heart; can it break a mind? He must have wrestled with this accusation all his adult life. Was *her* father, a prominent psychiatrist in Norway during her girlhood, who frequently brought the mentally ill home with him to study and work with, to blame? I was told that she was terrified by his patients, recoiled from them. Just as I had done upon meeting her.

The motherless children I've met have something in common other than just the motherless void in their lives. They feel—have felt during all their motherless years, including their adult years—without a rudder. When I became a mother myself I often wondered: what are the rules here? How do I *do* this? Mother was not there to show me, and so it was easy to slip into idealistic fantasy: She should be the Good Queen, able to rule, give wise moral counsel, yet teach me how to play Monopoly and Fish (maybe even Bridge!), how to give good gifts and send thank you notes and decorate for birthday parties. How to love.

In her absence I couldn't even conceive of such a person—except for a short time in Mrs. Cornwell. (Of course, Kirsten tried to mother me, but I opposed her, unkindly reminding her she was only my *sister*.) As I looked around at friend's mothers I decided that most were so flawed I was glad not to have one. I viewed all mothers with suspicion. Too harsh. Too preoccupied. Too scattered, undisciplined, unattractive. On and on the silent accusations fell, the verdicts written. Through the lens of my confused perceptions of my absent, disturbed, non-functioning mother I unconsciously locked in to a *prejudice*—against mothers!

In gravitating to Meredeth I chose a mother figure who was uniquely different, vibrant, fully alive to everything, and who warmly led me into regions that were toxic with fantasy. She became, for me (for she fostered the worship) a false god—or I should say goddess. To me, to Kirsten, and to the men she shamelessly seduced, her influence was hazardous to spiritual and relational health. She quested hard after the free life, but she unwittingly aligned herself with the wrong side, as so many in the New Age worldview do. What I received from Jesus I fervently long to pass on to her: redemption. How wonderful it will be to see the truly magnificent beauty that is Meredeth—unchained!

Forgiveness is a miracle beyond our wildest imagination, a supernatural transaction accompanied by the holy power of God and celebrated by all His angels. It blazes within the very nucleus of His love. He has shown me my own need of it in a thousand ways…including the need for forgiveness for holding onto that long, silent torment: my prejudice against mothers. And forgiveness of, in different ways, the four women who would have tried to fill that role but had to leave, or had to be left: Mother, Kirsten, Mrs. Cornwell—and Meredeth.

"Ask and you shall receive…" Pete had written in the Bible he gave me. They were Jesus' own words in Luke's Gospel. (Luke 11:9) I asked to be freed, and I received freedom. The prejudice is gone, and every child's mother looks different to me now. Including my own.

24

Consolation

My father lived into his nineties. In the years since my conversion a thousand prayers for him tore out of me, hit the ceiling—and his walls. I grieved for his increasing isolation and for the depression that clamped him shut against my love for him. For I did love him—passionately.

I often wondered what had transpired when Kathy went and spent two hours with my father, sharing the Gospel with an open Bible in her lap. All she would tell me as she departed his little apartment was, "He listened. He didn't argue." When I pressed her for more reasons to hope, she smiled and said simply, "We'll see."

But years later, some events gave me hope my prayers had gotten through. During the last few years of his life he had two experiences which were disturbing enough that he told me about them. Both were dreams.

The first occurred while he was 'camping out' with us in Santa Ynez, a golden valley east of Santa Barbara where I was then living. The years following his last film project in France, *The Longest Day*, had left him drifting, unsettled and lonely. At my pleading he had finally agreed to come and live nearby, even though he dubbed the Danish storybook town of Solvang "Danish Disneyland". He had found a lovely apartment there and was waiting for the current tenants to move out. His furniture was in storage. For several weeks, because of one complication after another with the recalcitrant tenants, he slept on our couch.

I woke one morning to hear him crying out in his sleep, a strangled, prolonged howl of terror. I jumped out of bed and ran into the living room. His unearthly cries gave me chills. I knelt by his side on the couch and gathered the covers up off the floor where they lay in a heap. His face was beaded with sweat and pale as death. I tucked the blankets around him and he awakened, startled and trembling.

"You were dreaming," I said.

"I couldn't breathe," he mumbled. His gnarled old hand plucked at the quilt. "It was a cobra. It was coming at my throat. It was right here, on my chest. Oh, God, it was hideous. I thought it would kill me."

He continued to repeat what he had experienced in that dream state, which is without time, endless in terror, more real than waking reality. Over and over he murmured, "I think I'm going to die."

I helped him out of bed and led him to the shower.

"I'll get you some coffee," I said.

There was no talking about things like that once they were over; I could never find words with which to approach him. He said nothing as he ate his boiled egg.

But the experience was so like what Helena had gone through. Almost exactly the same, actually, and I couldn't get it out of my mind. Was the enemy of his soul actually trying to kill him in his sleep? And was that enemy audacious enough to reveal himself in all his grotesque hideousness? Of course. I knew that. He doesn't hesitate to slide the shadow of his dark world over ours, like an eclipse.

So I found pen and paper and wrote my father a note. I knew his dream had profound significance. Dad was now well into his eighties. Death, if not exactly at the door, was lurking.

> *"I keep thinking about your terrible dream, Daddy,"* I wrote. *"But I need to tell you something. What you saw was evil. It was meant to scare you. But Dad, I know something. When death comes, it won't be a cobra facing you. It will be the most beautiful, happiest face you've ever seen: the face of Jesus. Because He loves you, and I have prayed for you. I love you, Daddy. Karin."*

I handed him the note after breakfast and shook in my boots while doing it. Never had I told him I loved him, even in writing. He didn't acknowledge the note—but somehow it didn't matter. He certainly had to have read it.

The second dream occurred just one year before his death.

I knocked on the door of his cozy apartment, opened it, and called out a greeting. He was sitting in his old armchair, pipe securely between his teeth as he gave me his usual wordless nod in response. He was in the middle of striking a match, probably the third or fourth in an effort to get that pipe going. It was nearly noon, and he was still in his bathrobe, and his hand was shaking hard.

"Do you have any coffee left?" I asked.

"Just about a cup, I think. You may have it."

"Did you sleep well?"

"Not particularly."

"How is your back?"

"Pretty stiff. It was hard to get out of bed."

"Is it better now?"

He shifted, finally getting some action from his pipe. He sucked in hard and blew the fragrant smoke my way. "Well, it should be, some. I've been up since four."

"Four! That's pretty early even for you."

"Well, yes." He fingered the tobacco in the bowl of the pipe and pulled his hand away in pain. It was hot and his fingers were singed. "That's when I had the damnedest dream I ever had in my life."

"What do you mean?"

"I mean, like nothing I've ever dreamed—or dreamed of dreaming—in my life."

He wasn't baiting me into an amusing story. He was frowning, eyes glittering with a mixture of wonder and fear. I asked him to tell me about it, because it was clear he wanted to.

"I dreamed my whole life. It was like reading a very long novel. How can that happen in the space of one night's dream? Every detail from beginning to end—in one dream. Most amazing thing I've ever…" He paused, laid the pipe in the ash tray I'd seen on that same table for thirty years. He looked down at his hands, which were still trembling, and shook his head.

"I tell you, there's never been anything like it. My life, the whole of it, nothing missing, in a dream."

"My whole life flashed before me…" rang through my head. The experience of a drowning person, the experience of one who is about to die. The revealing of every remembered—and every buried—truth.

A preview…a preparation…for the gift of redemption. Or of judgment.

My father was surrounded by Christians—real, living, breathing believers who loved him intensely. He was hemmed in by them and their testimonies on every side.

Like the manager of his apartment complex, whose husband came out of Alzheimers long enough to praise God and thank her for her love and faithful care one hour before his death. This was a testimony he received with unabashed tears.

And a Norwegian missionary named Rachel Mitchell, whose husband, Hubert, had found a three-inch nail in a can of mandarin oranges while ministering the Gospel in Indonesia (an answer to prayer while desperately trying to convey the crucifixion to a stone-age people who had never seen a nail). He was enabled to tell his story to Dad personally at a dinner I gave in Rachel's honor.

And more intimately, all my best friends who visited, brought gifts, ran errands. But especially my new husband, a man with a pastor's heart and irresistible tenderness toward my father—who—can you believe it?—adored him. Such tender love grew like a flower between them out of the parched ground of my father's old age. (When I had announced to Daddy that Wally had asked me to marry him, he pounded his fist on the arm of his old chair and exclaimed, "By God! That's the best news I ever heard!" I couldn't have agreed more—with both parts of the phrase!) Everyone surrounded him with the love that comes only from Jesus.

For the next year it was like watching the edges of an ice figure melt in the sun. An invisible seeping, a trickle. Silent, unrestrained tears, slipping. Contours changing, though not a word was said.

Then, on the very first day a visiting nurse I'd arranged to come and assist him arrived, he was found on the floor. He had been there, alive but helpless, for seven hours. He was rushed to the hospital. "He's weak, but stable," Dr. Pedersen said. "Are you wanting heroic interference in case of a crisis?" I didn't have to think long. I knew Dad wouldn't tolerate heroics.

"No," I answered. "I'll be there to help take care of him right after work." I had a part-time job in a small specialty market a mile away. Mentally I figured some temporary caregiving into my schedule.

"Hi, Daddy," I said as I walked into his room. "I'm here to have dinner with you."

He turned his head slightly and gave a little smile over bare gums. "That's good, Karin." His pillow was drenched with sweat, but his eyes sparkled at me.

I spoon fed him some broth. "I love you, Daddy," I said softly.

He nodded a little, eyes closed. "I was sitting in my chair, in the kitchen...having breakfast. It was like somebody lifted me up and threw me on the floor. I don't know how I got there..."

I stayed on my knees by the bed, my face close to his, and stroked his forehead. Freely I was touching him, loving him. Freely he was receiving me.

"I'll see you in the morning," I said when I finally left. "We'll get you out of here then." And I really believed it.

The next day, in the midst of a task, I was overwhelmed by a sense of urgency. I was alone in the market and couldn't leave. At that moment a pastor I'd become acquainted with walked in.

"Pastor Phillips," I cried, "I can't believe you're here! God be praised…you are desperately needed—right now." He looked at me without surprise, as if ready for any assignment. "Whatever it is, you've got it."

"My father—he's in the hospital. I can't go to him now, and besides, he needs *you*. Can you go? Right now?"

"Right now. What's his name?"

I told him Dad's name and the room number, and he was gone.

Two hours later he came back to report. "I can tell when someone is dying," he said gently. He waited a minute before going on, watching my face crumple.

"It's all right, Karin. He was sleeping deeply, so he probably didn't know I was there. But I prayed over him out loud this whole time. Even when the dying are unconscious the Word can get through." He smiled encouragingly and said, "And I promise you, he heard the Word."

◆   ◆   ◆

My father's death was followed by a third dream, this time given to a friend the night before his funeral.

"Last night I dreamed a scripture verse," Judy said. "That has never happened to me before. I had to turn on the light and look it up. It was for you…so that you would know." She handed me a slip of paper with the words *Job 33:14-30* on it. She smiled tenderly and put her arms around me. "I've never read those words in my life, Karin," she said.

At home on my bed I curled up in a tight ball, the way of the grieved, and opened my Bible. Through tears I read the words God had directed my friend to give me.

> *"For God speaks in one way, and in two, though man does not perceive it.*
>
> *In a dream, in a vision of the night, when deep sleep falls upon men,*
> *While they slumber on their beds,*
>
> *Then He opens the ears of men, and terrifies them with warnings,*
>
> *That He may turn man aside from his deed, and cut off pride from man.*
>
> *He keeps back his soul from the Pit, his life from perishing by the sword…*
>
> *His soul draws near the Pit, and his life to those who bring death.*
>
> *If there be for him an angel, a mediator, one of the thousand,*

To declare to man what is right for him;
And He is gracious to him, and says, 'Deliver him from going down into
    the Pit,
        I have found a ransom;
Let his flesh become fresh with youth; let him return to the days of his
    youthful vigor';
Then man prays to God, and He accepts him,
        He comes into His presence with joy.
He recounts to men his salvation, and he sings before men, and says:
I sinned, and perverted what was right,
        And it was not requited to me.
He has redeemed my soul from going down into the Pit,
        And my life shall see the light.'

Oh, pursued, pursued he was—
Pursued was she as well.
Pursued, pursued are we all—by redemption.

The End